TRAIL OF HOPE

TRAIL OF HOPE

THE STORY OF THE MORMON TRAIL

WILLIAM W. SLAUGHTER • MICHAEL LANDON

SHADOW MOUNTAIN • SALT LAKE CITY, UTAH

Library of Congress Cataloging-in-Publication Data

Slaughter, William W., 1952–
Trail of hope : the story of the Mormon Trail / by William W.
Slaughter and Michael Landon.
p.   cm.
Includes bibliographical references and index.
ISBN 1-57345-251-3
1. Mormon Trail—History. 2. Mormons—West (U.S.)—History.
3. Frontier and pioneer life—West (U.S.) 4. West (U.S.)—
Description and travel. I. Landon, Michael, 1953–   . II. Title.
F593.S57   1997
978—dc21   97-12727
                                                                                      CIP

Printed in Singapore

10   9   8   7   6   5   4   3   2   1

Bill dedicates this book to Sheri Eardley Slaughter, Viola Eardley, and his sister Nancy Jarratt.

Mike dedicates this book to Loretta, Cristy, and Laura.

CONTENTS

Opposite: Mormon emigrants near Coalville, Utah, c. 1867. Photographer: Charles W. Carter.

INTRODUCTION

THE WESTERN MIGRATION of more than five hundred thousand people via the overland trails is one of America's legendary stories. From 1806, when Lewis and Clark "opened" the West, until the 1869 joining of the railroads, these pioneers set out on trails leading to various points westward. Forsaking all they knew—sometimes leaving behind friends and family—the emigrants moved toward the unknown with hope for a new start and a better life.

Within this general migration is the story of some seventy thousand Mormon pioneers from Europe and America who traveled to their Zion in the Great Basin of the West—Salt Lake City. Most walked on foot in wagon trains, and during a four-year period, nearly three thousand pulled handcarts. Beginning with their expulsion from Nauvoo, Illinois, in 1846 and for the succeeding twenty-two years, the migration of the Mormon pioneers was a curious American saga in the settlement of the American West.

Opposite: THE OVERLAND TRAIL, *Albert Bierstadt, 1871.*

In 1847 the vanguard company of these religious refugees cut a trail into the vast frontier beyond the Missouri River. Led by the imposing, devout, and pragmatic Brigham Young, the Mormon pioneers trekked more than thirteen hundred miles into the arid Salt Lake Valley, arriving July 24. From this beginning the Mormons expanded out from Salt Lake City and eventually established three hundred and fifty settlements throughout what is now Utah, Idaho, Wyoming, Arizona, California, and Nevada.

Although the initial Mormon emigrants were *pushed* out of Nauvoo and into the West, subsequent groups were *pulled* to Zion in an effort to gather with fellow Saints. This was unusual in the movement west, as most emigrants traveled along the Santa Fe, Oregon, and California trails primarily for economic reasons—seeking fertile farmland or gold, or following the promise of work or business opportunities. The Mormons, on the other hand, gathered as a people hoping to worship and serve their God away from persecutors and misfortunes.

Mormon emigrants were well aware of the long-term religious significance of their efforts and sacrifices. Hannah Barwell Saunders, English emigrant of 1860, wrote in her reminiscence, "I desire to leave a record of those events and scenes through which I have passed that my children . . . may understand what their ancestors were willing to suffer, and did suffer patiently for the Gospel's sake. And, I wish them to know too, that what I now write is the history of hundreds of others, men, women, and children, who passed through like scenes at the same time we did. I also desire them to know that it was in obedience to the commandments of the true and living God, and with the assurance of an eternal reward—an exaltation to eternal life in His kingdom—that we suffered these things."[1]

The general outline of Hannah Saunders' odyssey was typical of many foreign Mormon emigrants who came after the initial 1847 vanguard group. She wrote, "On March 30, 1860, our ocean and overland journey to Utah began. We sailed from Liverpool. . . . We landed in Castle Garden, New York [City], May 1, 1860. . . . We went by board and rail to St. Joseph [Missouri] and from there took a boat up the Missouri River to Florence, Nebraska. We stayed in Florence until June 6th, when we began our journey with handcarts. . . . We reached the city [Salt Lake] on August 27, 1860."[2] However "typical" the general itinerary of a trip, the particulars of each individual's experience were unique to his or her own circumstances and personality as well as to such factors as weather, disease, leadership competence, and the amount of emigrant traffic on the trail.

For those who attempted the trip, the experience ranged from the tragic to the blasé. Nineteen-year-old Robert David Roberts, a member of the 1856 Edward Bunker Company, was saddled with the responsibility of helping his parents manage his five siblings. He wrote, "The suffering from heat and thirst were terrible and some of the people became so exhausted that they gave up and stopped their journey. . . . I was compelled to walk the last three hundred miles barefoot as my boots had worn completely out. . . . Several of the company died along the way from starvation and exposure."[3] On the other hand, Margaret Gay Judd [Clawson] admitted that for her as a seventeen-year-old emigrant in 1849, "everything was bright and beautiful." She wrote in her reminiscence, "I was young and healthy. All was color de rose for me. The responsibilities, anxieties and cares rested on my parents."[4] Some diarists delighted in the journey and the natural beauty around them. While in Weber Canyon, Utah, Lucy Marie Canfield Margetts wrote in her journal, "Oct 14th Tues [1862] A very

Above: PIONEER SISTERS MARY ELIZABETH AND EMMA CHASE, c. 1853. Photographer: Marsena Cannon.
Opposite: MORMON EMIGRANT CAMP AT WYOMING, NEBRASKA, 1866. Photographer: Charles R. Savage.

pleasant day Got started ½ past 8 Oclock. . . . Would not have missed coming this way for anything. I never saw such rocks they beat all that I saw in Echo Kanyan."[5]

Many non-Mormon contemporary writers, although critical of the Latter-day Saints' religion, were impressed with the Mormon trek. In 1857 Samuel Smucker wrote of the Mormons, "Any people who have the courage to travel over plains, rivers, and mountains . . . such probably

as cannot be travelled over in any other part of the world, to settle in a region which scarcely ever received the tread of any but the wild savage and beasts who roam the wilderness, must be possessed of indomitable energy which is but rarely met with."[6]

In noting the unique historic significance of the Mormon westwarding experience, twentieth-century American author Wallace Stegner wrote, "There are more than theological reasons for remembering the Mormon

pioneers. They were the most systematic, organized, disciplined, and successful pioneers in our history. . . . Where the Oregon emigrants and Argonauts bound for the gold fields lost practically all their social cohesion en route, the Mormons moved like the Host of Israel they thought themselves. Far from loosening their social organization, the trail perfected it."[7]

The Mormon trek is first and foremost a powerful story of people. These pioneers were not mere icons; they were individuals whose lives were filled with the full range of emotions, passions, and convictions we all feel. Their experiences revealed a mixture of Christian virtues and very human shortcomings. They willingly risked all, including their lives, to seek what they hoped would be a better way of life.

Some three thousand Mormon emigrants lost their lives during the twenty-two years of overland journeys. Others lost their faith either during the trek or following their arrival in the Great Basin. Incredibly, the majority did not die or lose their faith; in fact, they looked upon the trek as a "right of passage, the final, devoted, enduring act that brought one into the Kingdom" of God on earth.[8]

Mostly poor, they came from the eastern United States, Canada, England, the European continent, and a few from South Africa. They traveled on ships, canal boats, trains, and riverboats and then came on foot in wagon trains and handcart companies. An 1849 Florence,

Above: UNIDENTIFIED PIONEER COUPLE, *c. 1853.*
Photographer: Marsena Cannon.
Opposite: WAGONS EN ROUTE WEST.

Nebraska, observer described a Mormon wagon train in this way: "[They] began to bend their way westward over the boundless plains that lie between us and the Valley of the Great Salt Lake. Slowly and majestically they moved along, displaying a column of upwards of three hundred wagons, cattle, sheep, hogs, horses, mules, chickens, turkies, geese, doves, goats, &c., &c., besides lots of men, women and children. In this company was the Yankee with his machinery, the Southerner with his colored attendant—the Englishman with all kinds of mechanic's tools—the farmer, the merchant, the doctor, the minister, and almost every thing necessary for a settlement in a new country."[9]

This is the story of their trail of hope.

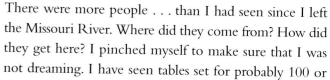

"Where Did They Come From?"

THE BEGINNING

IN THE SUMMER OF 1849, California-bound John Benson entered the Salt Lake Valley in time to observe the Mormon pioneers' Twenty-Fourth of July celebration. He captured his impressions in these words:

"This was a great day for the people in this vicinity. They were celebrating the second anniversary of their entrance into the valley. An immense amount of work and energy had been expended in preparing for the celebration. . . . It was estimated that 6000 to 8000 took dinner. I think 200 emigrants took dinner with them. All were urged to sit in. I hesitated but did so after two urgent invitations. The tables were spread with the greatest plenty and in taste and quantity not to be excelled. . . . As I walked away from the bower, I turned and looked back.

There were more people . . . than I had seen since I left the Missouri River. Where did they come from? How did they get here? I pinched myself to make sure that I was not dreaming. I have seen tables set for probably 100 or more, but here were tables for thousands. . . . How could they in so short a time with so small a beginning, have produced so much. It seems incredible. I take off my hat to those who planned and executed it."[1]

The 1846–1869 Mormon "trail of hope" to the Great Basin began during the great 1820 religious revivals in western New York. Concerned about which denomination to join, fourteen-year-old Joseph Smith retired to a secluded grove near his father's Palmyra

JOSEPH SMITH (1805–1844), c. 1842.

farm, where he knelt in prayer. He later wrote of his experience, "I . . . began to offer up the desires of my heart to God. . . . I saw a pillar of light exactly over my head, above the brightness of the sun, which descended gradually until it fell upon me. . . . I saw two personages, whose brightness and glory defy all description, standing above me in the air. One of them spake unto me, calling me by name and said—pointing to the other—'This is My Beloved Son. Hear Him!'" The boy was commanded to join no sect, "for they were all wrong."[2] This was the first in a series of divine visitations that not only changed his life and American religious history but would also eventually affect American western migration and settlement.

Describing one of these visitations, during the night of September 21, 1823, Smith wrote, "[The angel] called me by name, and said unto me . . . that God had a work for me to do; and that my name should be had for good and evil among all nations, kindreds, and tongues. . . . He said there was a book deposited, written upon gold plates, giving an account of the former inhabitants of this continent. . . . He also said that the fulness of the everlasting Gospel was contained in it."[3]

Once a year from 1823 until 1827, Smith visited a nearby hill where the plates were buried. Finally, on September 22, 1827, he was allowed to receive them and begin translating their ancient writings. The translation took three years, during which time Smith was often harassed and denounced as a blasphemer and a fraud.

With financial backing from Martin Harris, a prosperous farmer, Smith published the Book of Mormon in March 1830. The next month, more than thirty people

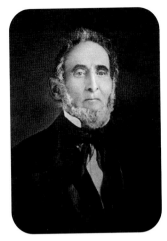

Right: SIDNEY RIGDON (1793–1876), counselor to Joseph Smith.
Below: LUCY MACK SMITH (1776–1855),
mother of Joseph Smith.

met to organize the Church of Christ (renamed The Church of Jesus Christ of Latter-day Saints in 1838); six were listed as official organizers. They selected the personable and energetic Smith to be their leader. He was also given the titles of seer, translator, and prophet.

Missionaries soon traveled west to spread the message of the new gospel. The mass conversion and baptism of 130 people in the Mentor-Kirtland area of northeast Ohio proved to be a catalyst for early, fast growth. From this group-conversion three significant converts, Sidney Rigdon, Frederick G. Williams, and Newel K. Whitney, would influence Smith and soon become church leaders. Along with success came increased resentment from non-Mormons—called "gentiles"—who distrusted Mormon claims to modern-day divine revelation. The "success and resentment" theme would continue to haunt these self-declared Saints well into their Utah years.

In 1831 Joseph Smith decided to assemble his Saints in the Kirtland, Ohio, area. Kirtland became the first in a series of gathering places. The concept of gathering came to Smith on September 1830 in a revelation in which he was told, "They shall be gathered in unto one place upon the face of this land."[4]

KIRTLAND TEMPLE, 1907. Photographer: George E. Anderson.

Nearly half of Smith's canonized revelations were received in the Kirtland vicinity. During this period he also worked on a new translation of the Bible; began to organize the administration of the Church; sent missionaries to England; established a colony near Independence, Missouri; and conducted the building of a temple. However, as ever-increasing numbers of converts moved to the Kirtland area, local "gentiles" grew hostile. On the night of March 24, 1832, while Joseph Smith and his wife, Emma, cared for their two adopted children, a mob burst open the door. "I

made a desperate struggle," Smith wrote. "They then seized me by the throat and held on till I lost my breath. After I came to, as they passed along with me, . . . I saw Elder Rigdon stretched out on the ground, whither they had dragged him by his heels. . . . They had concluded not to kill me, but to beat and scratch me well, tear off my shirt and drawers, and leave me naked. . . . They ran back and fetched the bucket of tar, . . . and one man fell on me and scratched my body with his nails like a mad cat, and then muttered out: *'G— d— ye, that's the way the Holy Ghost falls on folks!'* They then left me, and I attempted to rise, but fell again; I pulled the tar away from my lips, so that I could breathe more freely. . . . My friends spent the night in scraping and removing the tar, and washing and cleansing my body."[5]

Kirtland continued to be the Church's headquarters until apostasy, financial failures, and anti-Mormon persecution spurred an 1838 exodus from Kirtland to Missouri.

Previously, in June 1831, Smith had received a revelation directing him to go to Missouri, where the location of Zion—a perfected place of gathering—would be revealed. After he arrived in Missouri with a select group of followers, it was revealed to him that "the place for the city of Zion . . . which is now called Independence is the center place; and a spot for the temple is lying westward, upon a lot which is not far from the courthouse."[6] Smith returned to Ohio, and the Missouri Saints bought land, established businesses, and built homes. After a year of peace, non-Mormon neighbors in Missouri became hostile. In 1833 the Mormons, forced out of Independence, fled into neighboring Clay County. Their Missouri experience became a succession of conflicts with non-Mormons.

When Smith and the Kirtland Saints arrived in 1838, matters only grew worse, as Missouri was rife with rumors that the cohesive Saints intended to plunder and steal land from non-Mormons. By the fall of 1838, open conflicts grew in number and intensity. Missourians, mostly from southern states, saw the predominantly Yankee Mormons as invading abolitionists, further fueling an already heated situation.

On October 27 Governor Lilburn Boggs, siding squarely with anti-Mormons, issued his nefarious "Extermination Order." He wrote, "The Mormons must be treated as enemies and must be exterminated or driven from the state if necessary for the public peace."[7] Perhaps the worst encounter occurred three days after Boggs's order, during a declared truce, when two hundred Missouri militia made an unprovoked and brutal attack on the thirty Mormon families living at Jacob Haun's mill in Caldwell County. Women and children scattered into the woods. The men desperately tried to defend the village from inside a log shop that quickly became a death trap when the militia shot through the spaces between the logs. When the slaughter ended, seventeen Latter-day Saints (including a ten-year-old boy) and one friendly non-Mormon were dead; thirteen others were wounded. The panicked survivors hid

Left: THE OCTOBER 27, 1838, "EXTERMINATION ORDER," signed by Lilburn Boggs, forced the Mormons out of Missouri.
Right: LILBURN BOGGS (1796–1860), governor of Missouri.

the bodies of their loved ones in a well before fleeing to safety.

On October 31, 1838, the day after the Haun's Mill massacre, Joseph Smith and four others were arrested as they tried to negotiate peace. Then the prophet's brother Hyrum and Amasa Lyman were arrested and, along with the others, sentenced to die by firing squad. General Alexander Doniphan of the Missouri militia courageously refused to carry out the execution order, stating to his superior, "It is cold-blooded murder. I will not obey your order. . . . If you execute these men, I will hold you responsible before an earthly tribunal, so help me God."[8]

Nevertheless, Smith and five others were jailed, on charges of treason. They were incarcerated in the ironically named Liberty Jail, where conditions were dirty and cold, with straw on the floor for beds and "coarse and filthy food." During the winter of 1838–1839, in the absence of the jailed prophet, the pious and practical apostle Brigham Young directed the exodus of some ten thousand scattered, homeless, and harassed Mormons from Missouri. Across the Mississippi River, the citizens of Quincy, Illinois, compassionately aided the indigent Latter-day Saints. By April 22, 1839, Joseph Smith and his fellow prisoners were "allowed to escape" and soon joined the Saints gathering in Illinois.

Joseph Smith chose the swampy area of Commerce, Illinois, for the place to regroup the Saints. This town on the Mississippi River, renamed Nauvoo, served as Church headquarters from 1839 until 1846. In describing the new gathering place, Smith stated, "The place was literally a wilderness. The land was mostly covered with trees and bushes, and much of it so wet that it was with the utmost difficulty a footman could get through, and totally impossible for teams. Commerce was so unhealthful, very few could live there; but believing that it might become a healthful place by the blessing of heaven to the Saints, and no more eligible place presenting itself, I considered it wisdom to make an attempt to build up a city."[9]

Nauvoo soon became beautiful and prosperous. Methodist minister Samuel A. Prior visited Nauvoo in the spring of 1843 and reported, "Instead of seeing a few miserable log cabins and mud hovels . . . , I was surprised to see one of the most romantic places that I had visited in the west. The buildings, though many of them were small, and of wood, yet bore the marks of neatness which I have not seen equalled in this country. . . .

Opposite: HAUN'S MILL, *C.C.A. Christensen. During a truce between Mormons and Missourians, two hundred state militia made a brutal surprise attack on the isolated Mormon settlement at Haun's Mill. Above right:* GENERAL ALEXANDER DONIPHAN *(1808–1887), Missouri Militia. He refused to execute Joseph Smith and others. Engraved by Charles B. Hall. Right:* LIBERTY JAIL, *c. 1878. Joseph Smith and associates were jailed here from December 1838 to April 1839. Photographer: J. T. Hicks.*

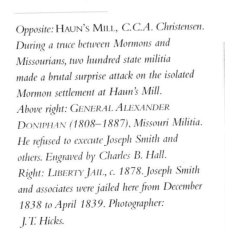

Here and there arose a tall majestic brick house, speaking loudly of the genius and untiring labor of the inhabitants, who have snatched the place from the clutches of obscurity, and wrested it from the bonds of disease; and in two or three short years, rescued it from dreary waste to transform it into one of the first cities in the west. . . . I passed on into the more active parts of the city, looking into every street and lane to observe all that was passing. I found all the people engaged in some useful and healthy employment. The place was alive with business."[10]

New converts from the East and England provided artisans and craftsmen to the growing city. By 1846 nearly

Above: VIEW OF NAUVOO.
Left: NAUVOO TEMPLE, *c. 1845. Photographer: possibly Lucian Foster.*

five thousand English converts had converged upon Nauvoo. At its zenith Nauvoo and the surrounding area was home for fifteen thousand Latter-day Saints.

During the Nauvoo period, the Mormon leader received new revelations, clarified various aspects of doctrine, stepped up the missionary effort in the United States and England, established the Female Relief Society, and began building the Nauvoo Temple.

Construction of the temple began in 1841. It occupied much of the Saints' emotional, spiritual, and physical energies until they left the city. The temple served as a centerpiece of Mormon religion where the Saints could perform sacred ceremonies and ordinances, covenanting as a symbol of their unity with each other and God. To ensure the completion of their "House of the Lord," many of the Saints were willing to forego the few material comforts frontier life provided. Elizabeth Kirby recounted in her reminiscence, "About this time [November 18, 1843], it was taught in our meetings that we would have to sacrifice our idols in order to be saved. I could not think of anything that would grieve me to part with in my possession, except Francis Kirby's [her deceased husband's] watch. So, I gave it to help build the Nauvoo Temple and everything else that I could possibly spare and the last few dollars that I had in the world, which altogether amounted to nearly $50."[11]

Neighboring gentiles grew resentful and antagonistic as Latter-day Saints prospered and as Smith centralized his religious and political power by serving as ecclesiastical leader, land agent, merchant, mayor, and leader of the municipal militia, the Nauvoo Legion. Rumors that Smith and select leaders were secretly teaching and practicing polygamy created additional dissension in the Mormon city. By the spring of 1844 a band of alienated Mormons, excommunicated Mormons, and anti-Mormons published the inflammatory *Nauvoo Expositor* in an effort to undermine Joseph Smith.

On June 10, 1844, at Smith's insistence, the Nauvoo City Council declared the *Nauvoo Expositor* a public nuisance and ordered it destroyed. Following the destruction of the press, Illinois governor Thomas Ford ordered Joseph Smith to be arrested and stand trial for treason. After a futile attempt to avoid imprisonment, Joseph Smith and his brother Hyrum turned themselves over to authorities and were jailed at nearby Carthage, Illinois.

Late on the afternoon of June 27, a mob of two hundred militiamen, their faces muddied as a disguise, charged into the jail and shot Joseph and Hyrum Smith to death. The Mormons were suddenly without their charismatic prophet.

Luman Shurtliff conveyed the feelings of all Latter-day Saints after the murder: "This Caused the Greatest Mourning of anything that has ever taken place with this people. A cloud of g[l]oom was spread over the People and Sorrow depicted in every face. On the

Above right: EMMA SMITH (1804–1879), widow of Joseph Smith, holding her son DAVID HYRUM SMITH, born five months after his father's martyrdom.
Right: HYRUM SMITH (1800–1844), brother and confidant of Joseph Smith.

28th When their Boddies ware brought into Nauvoo Most of the inhabitants went out and met them and accompanied them to the Mansion. Verry few of the Saints [who] visited their remains . . . [had not] droped a tear over those most Beloved Brethers. On viewing them I could but Call to mind the many Prophets and wise men Whose Blood had bin spiled by Wicked men to gratify the hatred of an assumed priesthood. My feelings ware at the time of our Sorrow that [I] would [have] rather Marched out with the L[e]gion with these men at our head onto the Prairie and faught the Whole United States until one party became extinct than to let these Brethren have Bin Murdered as they ware. But the [Church] Authorities that ware left said be stil and see the Salvation of God."[12]

The death of Joseph Smith left a void in the leadership of the Church. Anti-Mormons hoped the murders would put an end to what they thought was now a leaderless church. But Brigham Young, as president of the governing Quorum of Twelve Apostles, took the reigns. While some members split away over the question of

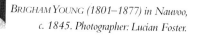

BRIGHAM YOUNG (1801–1877) in Nauvoo, c. 1845. Photographer: Lucian Foster.

leadership and plural marriage, most Saints rallied to Brother Brigham—the pragmatic Vermont-born carpenter.

During 1844 and 1845 Mormon-gentile relations grew increasingly hostile. In September 1845 Brigham Young, concerned for the safety of the Saints, publicly announced that they would leave Illinois in the spring of 1846.

To prepare for the westward exodus, Church leaders read Lansford Hastings's *The Emigrant's Guide to Oregon and California,* studied early descriptions by explorers Benjamin Bonneville and Charles Wilkes, interviewed scouts and trappers, and scrutinized the reports of John C. Fremont's 1842–1843 explorations. Brigham Young was determined to lead his people to an unsettled, isolated location—an area where no gentiles preceded them and, hopefully, none would follow. Texas, California, Oregon, and upper Washington were all considered and rejected. However, the protection of the valleys of the Great Basin interested Brother Brigham.

With this destination as their goal, Nauvoo became a hive of increased activity. The Latter-day Saints worked to complete their temple. They built wagons; gathered food; tried to sell property (usually in vain); collected tools, weapons, and clothing; and covenanted to help each other successfully complete the journey west. However, renewed threats forced an early and hasty departure before they were ready.

In January 1846 Brigham Young announced the preparation of several companies to leave at a moment's notice. On February 2 the decision was made to leave, and the first group crossed the Mississippi River during the wintry night of February 4. ✳

PACKIN' THE WAGON

For the Emigrants Leaving this Government Next Spring.
Each family consisting of five persons, to be
provided with

PIONEERS TRAVELED west in wooden wagons of various makes and origins. While many emigrants traveled in modified farm or work wagons, others, if they had the money, purchased wagons especially designed for the westward trip. Durable hardwoods, such as hickory and oak, were used in construction. To keep the weight of the wagon down, iron was limited to wheels, axles, and the connecting bars of the undercarriage. A typical wagon was approximately four feet wide, ten feet long, and topped with canvas waterproofed with linseed oil. The wagons could carry up to about twenty-five hundred pounds and were pulled by horses, mules, oxen, or even milk cows—sometimes a combination of these. However, the long-suffering ox was the animal of choice. Most travelers opted to walk rather than ride as rigs were constructed without springs to conserve on weight.

The items and provisions emigrants crammed into their wagons depended on individual preferences, needs, and resources. Advice—good and bad—was plentiful in various publications and from the ever-present experts selling over-priced provisions in outfitting towns. Throughout the twenty-two years of wagon emigration, Church leaders routinely gave sound and experience-based counsel to Mormon pioneers on what to bring and what to leave behind. For example, as the Latter-day Saints prepared to flee Illinois, the Church's October 29, 1845, *Nauvoo Neighbor* suggested the following list of provisions every family wagon should have:

1 good strong wagon,
well covered with a
light box
2 or 3 good yoke of oxen
between the age of 4
and 10 years
2 or more milk cows
1 or more good beeves
3 sheep if they can be
obtained
1000 lbs. of flour or other
bread or bread stuffs
in good sacks
1 good musket or rifle to
each male over the
age of 12 years
1 lb. powder
4 lbs. lead
1 lb. tea
5 lbs. coffee
100 lbs. sugar
1 lb. cayenne pepper
2 lbs. black pepper
½ lb. mustard
10 lbs. rice for each family
1 lb. cinnamon
½ lb. cloves

1 doz. nutmegs
25 lbs. salt
5 lbs. saleratus
10 lbs. dried apples
½ bushel of beans
A few lbs. of dried beef
or bacon
5 lbs. dried peaches
20 lbs. dried pumpkin
25 lb. seed grain
1 gal. alcohol
20 lbs. of soap each family
4 or 5 fish hooks and line
15 lbs. iron and steel
A few lbs. of wrought nails
One or more sets of saw
or grist mill irons
to company of 100
families
2 sets of pully blocks
and ropes to each com-
pany for crossing rivers
1 good seine and hook for
each company
From 25 to 100 lbs. of
farming and
mechanical tools

Cooking utensils to consist
of a bake kettle, frying
pan, coffee pot, and
tea kettle
Tin cups, plates, knives,
forks, spoons, and
pans as few as will do
A good tent and furniture
to each 2 families

Clothing and bedding
to each family not to
exceed 500 pounds
Ten extra teams
for each company
of 100 families

N.B. In addition to the above list, horse and mule teams,
can be used as well as oxen. Many items of comfort and
convenience will suggest themselves to a wise and provident
people, and can be laid in in season; but none should
start without filling the original bill.[13]

How a family packed a wagon depended on their personalities and needs and the amount and kinds of provisions brought. Bathsheba Smith, pioneer of 1849, gives a glimpse into her wagon: "On this journey my wagon was provided with projections, of about eight inches wide, on each side of the top of the box. The cover, which was high enough for us to stand erect, was widened by these projections. A frame was laid across the back part of our wagon, and was corded as a bedstead; this made our sleeping very comfortable. Under our beds we stowed our heaviest articles. We had a door in one side of the wagon cover, and on the opposite side a window. A step-ladder was used to ascend to our door, which was between the wheels. Our cover was of 'osnaburg,' lined with blue drilling. Our door and window could be opened and closed at pleasure. I had, hanging up on the inside, a looking-glass, candlestick, pin-cushion, etc. In the centre of our wagon we had room for four chairs, in which we and our two children sat and rode when we chose. The floor of our traveling house was carpeted, and we made ourselves as comfortable as we could under the circumstances."[14]

Many pioneers overestimated the amount of cargo they could haul. As the long journey weakened and wearied the oxen, loads were lightened. Such heirlooms as prized furniture, book collections, china, and pianos were often abandoned along the trail. Sometimes precious items were left along the trail with the hope of picking them up at a later date. Such was the case with the Kimball family in 1847. As they approached the mountains, they unloaded their piano (shown below left), dug a large hole, wrapped the piano in buffalo skins, carefully placed it in the hole, and then covered it with dirt. The following spring an ox team transported it to Salt Lake City.

The key to surviving the westward trek was to take enough but not too much. Following a list of needed provisions, Lansford Hastings wrote in his emigrant guide, "It would, perhaps, be advisable for emigrants, not to encumber themselves with any other, than those just enumerated; as it is impracticable for them, to take all the luxuries, to which they have been accustomed."[15] However, he was assuming emigrants were acquainted with luxuries; many, perhaps most, were not. In any case, careful planning enhanced the chances for a safe arrival in the Great Basin.

"A Continuous Mud Hole"

THE IOWA TREK

LORENZO YOUNG, as he prepared to leave Nauvoo in February 1846, expressed the feelings of thousands of Latter-day Saints who faced the same uncertain future: "Now fixing to leave Our Home and al[l] we have except what too wagons can Draw and our Place of Destenation We know not."[1] The epic story of the Mormon exodus from Nauvoo began with the march across Iowa by the self-proclaimed "Camp of Israel." Comparing themselves to the Old Testament children of Israel wandering in the deserts of Sinai, this advance company numbered between two and three thousand people and included much of the Church leadership. They sought to establish a route to a yet-unknown destination in the West that the main body of the Church would follow.

Planning for the move west had been in process for some time, but no one anticipated a midwinter departure. As these first members prepared to cross the Mississippi River, temperatures fell and the water froze, allowing many to cross a river of ice. Regarding the winter exodus, their leader Brigham Young later wrote:

"The fact is worthy of remembrance that several thousand persons left their homes in midwinter and exposed themselves without shelter, except that afforded by a scanty supply of tents and wagon covers, to a cold which effectually made an ice bridge over the Mississippi river which at Nauvoo is more than a mile broad.

"We could have remained sheltered in our homes had it not been for threats and hostile demonstrations of our enemies, who, notwithstanding their solemn agreements, had thrown every obstacle in our way, not respecting either life, or liberty, or property; so much so that our only means of avoiding a rupture was by starting in midwinter."[2]

After crossing the Mississippi to Montrose, the first Mormon refugees traveled west and camped on Sugar Creek, some seven to nine miles from the river. There the Camp of Israel remained for several weeks. With no consensus on a route, and faced with the overwhelming task of organizing thousands of people for the journey in the

midst of a harsh winter, members of the Camp of Israel endured the delay, finally departing on March 1.

Many would-be immigrants, fearful of being left behind, created additional problems by crossing the Mississippi totally unprepared to make the journey, exasperating Brigham Young and other Church leaders. Demand inflated prices for ox teams and wagons while the growing supply of real estate in Nauvoo caused land prices to plummet. Many Latter-day Saints, particularly those who left in subsequent months, found it impossible to unload their property at any price, and if they could, finding wagons and teams proved difficult. As one Hancock County newspaper reported, it seemed impossible for the venture to succeed:

"We visited the Camp before it broke up on the opposite side of the River, and, with other strangers, were highly interested in the romantic and exciting display of border enterprise. It bore the appearance of a movable town, the wagons and tents being arranged on either side of large streams, and public spaces left for the cattle . . . [and] such broken down nags as are attached to this expedition. If they ever reach California, their dependence must be partly upon slow traveling and partly upon miracle—but chiefly upon the latter."[3]

William Pace wrote, "Our camp was made in the snow about 8 inches deep and was a rather uncomfort-

Top: LORENZO YOUNG (1807–1895), pioneer, brother of Brigham Young. Center: WILLIAM PACE (1832–1907). Bottom: ABNER BLACKBURN (1828–1904), pioneer and frontiersman, c. 1868.

able introduction into camp life without tent or any shelter save it be a wagon cover made from common sheeting. Here we stayed for some time waiting the arrival of all those who could possibly supply themselves with teams."[4] Even when teams were available, they were often unbroken and hard to control. A young Abner Blackburn wrote, "I trained the cattle round a day or two before we started on our higeria [hegira]; loaded up with live stock and their effects. . . . Well, we started and such a time I had with that team of raw unbroken wild steers. I was in the road part of the time and that was when I was crossing it."[5]

Many of the refugees made efforts to bring a sense of normalcy to their lives while waiting out the delays at Sugar Creek. Helen Kimball Whitney wrote, "Camplife in February [1846] was quite a novel experience. . . . The band played every evening. I there took my first lesson in the Danish waltz. The weather was so cold that it was impossible to keep warm with[out] exercise."[6] As they traveled west, William Pitt's Brass Band continued to play for the camp in the evening and for audiences in the towns of Farmington and Keosauqua.[7]

When the Camp of Israel left Sugar Creek, they traveled northwest, crossing the Des Moines River at Bonaparte, where they ground wheat at a local gristmill before continuing their journey. Continuing their travels northwest, they came to Richardson's Point (Richard's Point in some journals) on the western edge of Van Buren County, where once again harsh weather halted travel. Erastus Snow, a Church apostle, later wrote of the difficulties caused by the weather:

"The company . . . succeeded in reaching a point of

C.1885.

Sugar Creek

timber 20 miles above called Richardson's Point. . . . Here they were compelled to remain until the 16th inst. During this time it rained almost incessantly and the roads were rendered impassable, and our encampment being trod into a perfect Mortar bed by ourselves & stock, was far from being a pleasant one."[8]

Here they spent ten days in an unceasing downpour that contributed to two deaths. During the delay, at least

SUGAR CREEK, *C.C.A. Christensen. Poorly provisioned Saints camped at this Iowa stream after their hasty exodus from Nauvoo.*

thirty of the one hundred eighty men serving the camp as a military guard returned to Nauvoo to help their families prepare to travel west.[9]

Richardson's Point brought perspective to many about the sacrifices they were making. To Eliza R. Snow, the simple kindness of a friend held added significance in light of their wilderness surroundings: "March 11, Richardson's Point. My Good friend Sister Markham brought me a slice of beautiful, white light bread and butter, that would have done honor to a more convenient bakery than an out-of-door fire in the wilderness."[10]

With improving weather, they left Richardson's Point and continued west-northwest to Drakesville. At Drakesville the Camp of Israel changed direction from their intended course and veered far to the south for an essential reason.[11] Erastus Snow wrote:

"We journeyed up the Fox river till we struck what is called the old Mormon trace (it being the trail of a party of brethren who made their escape from their enemies in Far West, Mo. in November 1838). . . . Finding it impracticable to haul grain for our teams, in the bad condition of the roads and it being too early to sustain them upon grass we thought it expedient to deviate from the direct course which we had intended to travel and bear further south so as to keep near the border settlements where we could obtain feed for our teams. In pur-

Above: WILLIAM PITT *(1813–1873), whose brass band entertained the Saints and non-Mormon communities in Iowa.*
Left: ELIZA R. SNOW *(1804–1887), Mormon poetess and leader. Photographer: Charles R. Savage.*

suance of this council we took the old Mormon trace, crossed Fox River a few miles above Bloomfield & followed it to the Ford of the Chariton River."[12]

Whether the border settlements Erastus referred to were in Missouri or Iowa is unclear, as the boundary between the two states was hotly disputed at the time. Following the old Mormon trace toward Missouri exposed the company to possible harassment, a necessary risk given the need to provide for their stock. This southern detour did not last, and subsequent Mormon trains took a shorter and more direct route west.

At the Chariton River the Camp of Israel stalled again. Apostle Orson Pratt recorded:

"The heavy rains had rendered the prair[i]es impassable; and our several camps were very much separated from each other. We were compelled to remain as we were for some two or three weeks, during which time our animals were fed upon the limbs and bark of trees, for the grass had not yet started, and we were a number of miles from any inhabited country, and therefore, it was very inconvenient to send for grain. The heavy rains and snows, together with frosty nights, rendered our situation very uncomfortable. Our camps were now more perfectly organized, and captains were appointed over hundreds, over fifties, and over tens, and over all these, a president and counsellors, together with other necessary officers."[13]

Back at Sugar Creek in February, Brigham Young had organized the Camp of Israel similarly, stating, "It will not do to start off helter-skelter without order and decorum— if we should, but few would reach the place of destination.

Continued on page 33

HITCHIN' & CONTROLLIN' THE WAGON

Even though pioneers used horses, mules, and an occasional milk cow to pull their wagons, oxen were the preferred draft animal of western migration. Strong, hardy, and relatively long-suffering, they were also cheaper to purchase and maintain than horses or mules.

Simple wooden yokes around the neck of the oxen allowed them to pull the wagon. To "drive" the ox team, a person walked on the left side just behind the lead oxen, urging them along with the aid of a whip or prod, all the while shouting commands of either "haw" to turn left or "gee" to turn right.

Most nights on the trail, the cattle were left free to graze under the watchful eye of the night guards, yet many would wander far from camp in their search for feed. In the morning, the oxen were gathered and driven into the corral of circled wagons, sorted out, and then yoked. Emigrant farmers accustomed to working with cattle readily took to the task of yoking and driving the oxen. However, European and American urban emigrants were in for a new experience.

In *Route from Liverpool to Great Salt Lake Valley,* published in 1855, the author gives this account of emigrants learning to work with their beasts of burden: "Then began the yoking of refractory cattle, and the initiation of 'greenhorns' into the art and mystery of teaming. . . . The cattle were driven into the 'corral,' and then, with yokes and bows in hand, it was the business of the teamsters to catch and yoke their teams, but,

unfortunately, they did not know their business. Many of them had never touched an ox before, so that the wide-spreading horns of the untrained steers seemed to produce a most uncomfortable nervousness. The consequence was, that Elders Miller and Cooley had to do nearly all the work. . . . The road was rather rough, and so were the cattle, and, in the hands of raw teamsters, nearly unmanageable. Elder Miller was here and there and every where, giving untrained teams, and teamsters in training, many practical illustrations of the art. 'Geeing' and 'hawing' were most forcibly taught. . . . During the first few

Yoking a Wild Bull, *William H. Jackson.*

days the teams and teamsters were constantly at variance. Nearly every man had the worst team in the company! Some steers would not 'gee,' others would do nothing else, and then would come an appeal . . . —'O, brother Miller, do come here and try to make my lead steer 'haw,' for the stupid brute does nothing but run away from me.' . . . Elder Miller would bring the oxen back, and with his good-humoured smile say—'Now you are a pretty teamster, ain't you, to go and place your ugly body and long dangling whip right before their eyes, instead of keeping back as you ought.' Then away he would go, shouting and hallooing to a man, who, in defiance of the sacred laws of teaming, would be driving on the right hand side of his team instead of the left."[14]

Abner Blackburn succinctly speaks volumes of the travails of learning to drive a team of oxen: "Such a time I had with that team of raw unbroken wild steers. I was in the road part of the time and that was when I was crossing it."[15]

The voices of the "geeing" and "hawing" teamsters as well as the calls of night watchmen were prominent sounds on the trail. On August 9, 1851, Emily Smith Hoyt wrote, "This morning I felt better than usual. I think the Watchman, Herdsmen and Teamsters have somewhat abated their wo! Who! woa! whoah! Gee! gua! gee-awff! and every other sound in their power to make."[16]

By and by the greenhorns and oxen became used to each other's peculiarities and eventually trained each other. Oxen, after their initial stubbornness, became dependable laborers. It was not unusual for pioneers to develop a love for these animals on whom so much depended. As a nine-year-old, Joseph F. Smith endured the difficult adult tasks of yoking, unyoking, caring for, and driving his mother's team of oxen across the plains in 1848 (his father, Hyrum Smith, had been murdered with the prophet Joseph Smith in 1844). Years later, Smith remembered, "My team leaders' names were Thom and Joe. . . . Thom was trim built, active, young, and more intelligent than many a man. Many times while traveling sandy or rough roads, on long, thirsty drives, my oxen were lowing with the heat and fatigue. I would put my arms around Thom's neck and cry bitter tears! That was all I could do. Thom was my favorite and best and most willing and obedient servant and friend. He was choice!"[17]

Many animals became wise to the daily ritual as attested by seventeen-year-old 1849 emigrant Margaret Judd [Clawson]: "One cow in our team was very intelligent; in fact, she was so bright that she used to hide in the willows to keep from being yoked up, but when Father found her and yoked her she was a good worker."[18]

Mormon pioneers who learned the art of driving a team and, more important, who carefully tended to their team's health optimized chances for a successful end to their journey. Those who abused their animals either through harsh treatment or neglect were putting themselves in harm's way.

Continued from page 30

. . . When we get all the camp together then we will number Israel and organize them into companies of tens, of fifties and of hundreds and place captains over them."[19]

Organizing the camp a second time was due in part to the shifting composition of the Camp of Israel. Speaking of the camp at the Chariton, Sarah Rich wrote, "Here at this

place . . . many of our pioneers returned to Nauvoo to prepare to bring on their families and friends."[20]

One of the returning "pioneers" gave the following account to the *Hancock Eagle:*

"The Camp of Israel

"This is the 'title and address,' which has been adopted by the company of Mormons now on their way Westward. A mail carrier arrived here on Monday last from the Camp, and reported the pioneer party . . . as having crossed the tributaries of the Chariton, over 150 miles

Mormon pioneers fleeing Nauvoo.
From T.B.H. Stenhouse, The Rocky Mountain Saints.

distant. By this time they are probably on the banks of the Missouri.

"Thus far, everything has gone favorably with the exception of the breaking down of a few overladen wagons. The party is in good health and spirits—no dissensions exist; and the Grand Caravan moves slowly and steadily and peacefully. Their progress has been materially retarded by the want of fodder for their live stock;—the grass not having fairly started, reduced them to the necessity of laboring for the farmers on the route to supply the deficiency.

"They travel in detached companies, from five to ten miles apart and in point of order, resemble a military expedition."[21]

Regardless of the privations Mormon refugees suffered while crossing Iowa, the rhythm of life continued. Zina Huntington Young wrote poignantly of giving birth:

"On the bank of the Chariton an incident occurred ever eventful in the life of woman. I had been told in the temple that I should acknowledge God even in a miracle in my deliverance in woman's hour of trouble, which hour had now come. We had traveled one morning about five miles, when I called for a halt in our march. There was but one person with me— Mother Lyman, the aunt of George A. Smith; and there on the bank of the Chariton I was delivered of a fine son. . . . I journeyed on. But I did not mind the hard-

DRAWINGS DEPICTING MORMON EXODUS SCENES IN IOWA. *Heber C. Kimball's 1846 diary.*

ship of my situation, for my life had been preserved, and my babe seemed so beautiful."[22]

Leaving the Chariton, the Camp of Israel continued west, reaching Locust Creek. Sarah Rich wrote with some understatement, "We left the Chariton on our march towards the Rocky Mountains, leaving all the settlements behind, so from there on we had to pick our way without any road, only as we made it."[23]

In this vicinity William Clayton penned the famous Mormon hymn "Come, Come Ye Saints" after learning that his wife Diantha, still in Nauvoo, had given birth to a healthy baby boy. On April 15 he wrote in his journal:

"This morning Ellen Kimball came to me and wishes me much joy. She said Diantha has a son. I told her I was afraid it was not so, but she said Brother Pond had received a letter. I went over to Pond's and he read that she had a fine fat boy on the 30th ult. [ultimo: of the preceding month], but she was very sick with ague and mumps. Truly I feel to rejoice at this intelligence but feel sorry to hear of her sickness. . . . In the evening . . . [several] persons retired to my tent to have a social christening. . . . We named him William Adriel Benoni Clayton. . . . This morning I composed a new song—'All is Well.' I feel to thank my heavenly father for my boy and pray that he will spare and preserve his life and that of his mother and so order it so that we may soon meet again."[24]

At Locust Creek, Church leaders adopted a plan to establish waystations, plant crops, and prepare for the thousands following behind. The detour south, while provid-

ing the needed feed and provisions, had drawbacks. Brigham Young stated, "We consider it wisdom to avoid the [southern Iowa and northern Missouri] settlements as much as possible for there seems to be only one disposition which is universal amongst the inhabitants in this region, and that is to speculate out of us as much as possible, and we mean to defeat them."[25]

Leaving Locust Creek, the company pursued a more northerly track, camping at a place where they decided to establish a permanent settlement. Apostle Parley P. Pratt later

Left: ZINA D. H. YOUNG (1821–1901) with stepchildren WILLARD AND PHOEBE YOUNG, c. 1860. Right: WILLIAM CLAYTON (1814–1879), author of song "Come, Come Ye Saints," and his eighth wife, MARIA LOUISA LYMAN CLAYTON (1849–1877), c. 1866.

wrote, "Here we enclosed and planted a public farm of many hundred acres and commenced settlement, for the good of some who were to tarry and of those who should follow us from Nauvoo. We called the place 'Garden Grove.'"[26]

Zera Pulsipher accompanied Pratt on the assignment "to look for a location for the poor, and such as could not go on." He wrote, "We found a grove of timber and called it Garden Grove, a convenient place for a settlement. I then unloaded my wagon and delivered my load of flour and bacon and went back to look after my family."[27]

The struggle to cross Iowa and the less-than-perfect conditions at Garden Grove taxed even the most hardy, and tempers often ran short. Allen Stout recorded, "About these times the rattle snakes bit a good many of our animals and there was a great deel of sickness in camp on account of the great exposure the saints were forced to undergo. . . . There was great want of bread in camp, so that we were oppressed on every hand but we cried to the Lord who herd our Prares and we wer fed by his all bountiful hand but some showed out theire evil harts by there meen intreegs and shelfishness."[28]

West of Garden Grove, Church leaders soon established a second, larger settlement called Mount Pisgah. In his autobiography, Parley P. Pratt related:

"Being pleased and excited at the varied

PARLEY P. PRATT (1807–1857), c. 1853.
Early convert, author, and apostle who was murdered
in Arkansas. Photographer: Marsena Cannon.

beauty before me, I cried out, 'this is *Mount Pisgah.*' . . . It was now late in May, and we halted here to await the arrival of the President and council. In a few days they arrived and formed a general encampment here, and finally formed a settlement, and surveyed and enclosed another farm of several thousand acres. This became a town and resting place for the Saints for years, and is now known on the map of Iowa as a village and post-office named '*Pisgah.*'"[29]

Mount Pisgah served as the temporary Church headquarters from May 18 until the end of the month. The Camp of Israel continued west on June 2, minus those who stayed at Garden Grove and Mount Pisgah. Traveling became much easier as roads were now drier and feed readily available. The camp arrived at the Missouri River on June 14. It had taken four months to travel from Nauvoo to Mount Pisgah, about one hundred seventy-five miles. With the improved weather, the last ninety miles from Mount Pisgah to the Missouri River took only about twelve days.

However, the main body of the Church, ten thousand strong and strung out all across Iowa, trailed the Camp of Israel. The full scope of this unprecedented exodus was vividly described in Illinois newspapers of 1846:

"Late From the Mormon Camp

"*Hancock Eagle,* of Friday last, notices the arrival there of Mr. S. Chamberlain, who left the most distant camp of the Mormons at Council Bluffs on the 26th, and on his route passed the whole line of Mormon emigrants. He says that the advance company of the Mormons, with whom were the Twelve [Apostles], had a train of one thousand wagons, and were encamped on the east bank of the Missouri River, in the neighborhood of the Council Bluffs. They were employed in the construction of boats, for the purpose of crossing the river.

"The second company had encamped temporarily at station No. 2, which has been christened Mount Pisgah. They mustered about three thousand strong, and were recruiting [resting and feeding] their cattle preparatory to a fresh start. A third company had halted for a similar purpose at Garden Grove, on the head waters of Grand river, where they have put in about 2000 acres of corn for the benefit of the people in general. Between Garden Grove and the Mississippi river, Mr. Chamberlain counted over one thousand wagons en route to join the main bodies in advance.

"The whole number of teams attached to the Mormon expedition, is about three thousand seven hundred, and it is estimated that each team will average at least three persons and perhaps four. The whole number of souls now on the road may be set down in round numbers at twelve thousand. From two to three thousand have disappeared from Nauvoo in various directions. Many have left for Council Bluffs by the way of the Mississippi and Missouri rivers—others have dispersed to parts unknown; about eight hundred or less still remain in Illinois. This comprises the entire Mormon population that once flourished in Hancock [County]. In their palmy days they probably numbered between fifteen and sixteen thousand souls, most of whom are now scattered upon the prairies, bound for the Pacific slope of the American continent."[30]

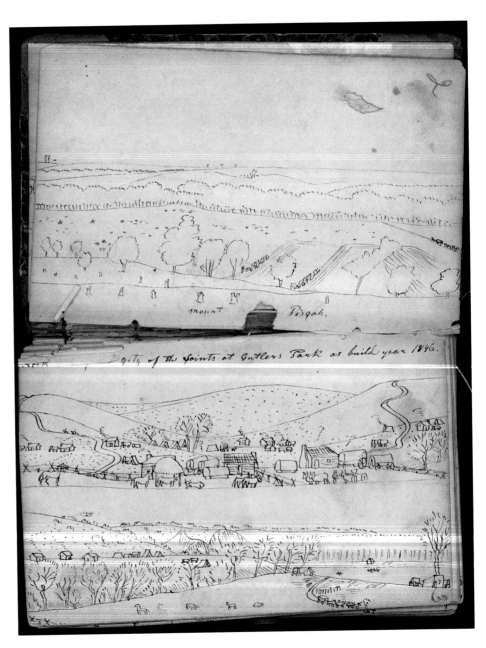

MOUNT PISGAH and CUTLERS PARK. Heber C. Kimball's 1846 diary.

Also traveling behind the Camp of Israel, Benjamin Critchlow described his arrival at Garden Grove: "A large portion of our journey in Iowa seemed to me to be a continuous mud hole. We arrived at Garden Grove . . . where the first company had halted on their journey, to break ground and plant crops for those that were not able to come or proceed farther during that year. Father camped for some weeks by the side of William Middleton's family, where I became acquainted with Charles F. Middleton, a boy some older than myself. He was engaged in training a yolk of yearling calves that were to grow into oxen and perhaps assist them as a team in their journey farther west."[31]

Also among the thousands following behind the Camp of Israel was Louisa Barnes Pratt, who on June 15 described the fledgling community of Mount Pisgah:

"June 15th [1846] We have at last arrived at Mount Pisgah. The tents are scattered everywhere. Poor people here; they are in the sun without houses. I pity them. May the Lord reward them for all their sacrifices. I have just

returned from a long walk, having made a survey of the place. On the Bluffs is a beautiful grove of oak trees; beneath the towering branches we can pitch our tents and be sheltered from the sun's scorching rays. Several little cabins begin to make their appearance. The post office is laughable, a little log pen, 10 x 8, covered with bark."[32]

Some of the Saints in Iowa returned to Nauvoo to retrieve family members. Philemon Merrill wrote:

"President Young told me to take my team and return to Nauvoo and get my family. My team had hauled some of the Church Records. I found on my return that my wife had been confined and had given birth to a nice little girl. . . . When she was only a week old I put my all into a wagon and started across the River again. And when I got across the River I traded one of my horses and got a yoke of oxen to strengthen my team, putting my horses on ahead of my oxen. My draft horse was at Mount Pisgah, where with my Father, Mother and four brothers with three brothers-in-law, we went to work and put up three log houses, thinking to stop there for a season. But finally we were all united to go on, we left our houses for others to inhabit."[33]

John Pulsipher, one of the later emigrants, commented on the condition of the thousands who had left Nauvoo: "We arrived at the headquarters of the Camp of Israel on the west side of the Missouri River. This was the 1st of September. The Saints were scattered from Nauvoo to this place and many had not started because they could get no teams."[34]

ZERA (1789–1872) and MARY BROWN PULSIPHER (1798–1886). Photographer: George E. Anderson.

BATTLE OF NAUVOO, *C.C.A. Christensen.*
In September 1846 the few hundred sick and poor Mormons
remaining in Nauvoo were forced out by well-armed marauders.

Like Pulsipher, most Latter-day Saints escaped from Nauvoo by the end of August, signaling the start of the saddest chapter in the exodus across Iowa. It involved the last to leave, the "poor saints" as they were known, who were financially or physically incapable of traveling west without assistance. In September 1846 mobs attacked the remaining citizens of Nauvoo in what came to be known as the "battle of Nauvoo." Numbering less than a thousand, the remaining Mormons were violently forced out of the city and across the river. Thomas Bullock, writing to his friend Willard Richards in Iowa, described his family's sickness and the circumstances of the last Latter-day Saints in the city:

"I have been shaking every day for the last month and can scarce write any. I received yours of Aug. 14 while shaking at ten or twelve knots an hour—and as you told me not to perform any impossibilities—I have hitherto found it an impossibility to sell my house and lot—but the very next morning I wrought [a] miracle, in giving it away for one hundred dollars. The only obstacle [to] the successful termination of my miracle is, I have not yet got the hay—you may rest assured I have done, and will do my best to *come*. I have a very kind neighbor, who, as quick as he heard I had bargained for the disposal of my place, began to run it down, and has caused Mr. Bolander to waver about completing his purchase. May the Lord reward him for it. . . .

"Even my little boy says, 'dadda I wish we were out of this country, for when I've done shaking I can get nothing to eat'—we have all been 'shake, shake, shaking' more or less for the last five weeks. A fortnight ago, I, Henrietta,

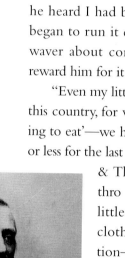

& Thomas Henry were not expected to live thro the day . . . and if it had not been for a little Charity—and Henrietta selling her clothes we should all have died of starvation—it will almost be a miracle if you see little Willard alive for he has fallen away dreadful this week—and if you was to see me and my family at this moment, you would say we had either been whitewashed or had risen out of our graves—we have not the least idea where our next meal is to come from. . . .

Thomas Bullock (1816–1885).

"There have been . . . many Saints who were preparing as fast as they could to go to the west—who have gone to the grave. Many literally dying for want—whole families are sick—and not one to help the other—two or three dying in a house—great difficulty in getting coffins and then to be buried by strangers—there is not one house in this neighborhood, but there has been sickness in it. . . .

"In addition to all this, the Mob is within five miles . . . about 5 or 600 Strong & with 8 cannon—those Saints who are well are in the woods this side of Joseph's farm—the Cannon were roaring about 5 P.M. yesterday but I have not yet heard of any casualties on our side."[35]

Bullock chronicled the final death throes of the once-vibrant Nauvoo. The cancer of persecution and conflict started sapping the city's strength even before the martyrdom of Joseph Smith in June 1844. The terminal stage was signaled when its Mormon population began streaming out of Nauvoo, across the Mississippi, and into Iowa the previous February. At first a trickle, the exodus became a flood by late spring and early summer until only these very poor and weak remained.

After visiting a deserted Nauvoo, non-Mormon Thomas L. Kane crossed the Mississippi and found the "poor saints" on the west bank. He wrote:

"Here, among the docks and rushes, sheltered only by the darkness, without roof between them and the sky, I came upon a crowd of several hundred human creatures, whom my movements roused from uneasy slumber upon the ground. . . . Dreadful indeed, was the suffering of these forsaken beings; bowed and cramped by cold and sunburn, alternating as each weary day and night dragged on, they were, almost all of them, the crippled victims of disease. They were there because they had no homes, nor hospitals, nor poor house, nor friends to offer them any. They could not satisfy the feeble cravings of their sick; they had not bread to quiet the fractious hunger-cries of their children. Mothers and babes, daughters and grandparents, all of them alike, were bivouacked in tatters, wanting even covering to comfort those whom the sick shivers of fever were searching to the marrow. These were Mormons, famishing in Lee county, Iowa, in the fourth week of the month of September, in the year of our Lord 1846. . . . They were, all told, not more than six hundred forty persons who were thus lying on the river flats. But the Mormons in Nauvoo and its dependencies had been numbered the year before at over twenty thousand. Where were they? They had last been seen, carrying in mournful trains their sick and wounded, halt and blind to disappear behind the western horizon, pursuing the phantom of another home. Hardly anything else was known of them and people asked with curiosity—what had been their fate, what their fortune!"[36]

Brigham Young, desperate to bring these last, impoverished Saints west, wrote of his mounting frustrations:

Above: BRIGHAM YOUNG, c. 1850. Photographer: Marsena Cannon.

"The saints have crowded on us all the while, and have completely tied our hands by importuning and saying: Do not leave us behind. Wherever you go, we want to go, be with you, and thus our hands and feet have been bound which has caused our delay to the present time. . . . They are afraid to let us go on and leave them behind, forgetting that they have covenanted to help the poor away at the sacrifice of all their property."[37]

Many of the Saints had made a covenant in the Nauvoo Temple not to forget the poor and to do all they could to bring them west. Finally, the Church leadership requested many to return to Nauvoo and bring out the poor or to remain at Garden Grove and Mount Pisgah to build up the farms for those traveling behind. Eventually the "poor saints" arrived at the Missouri River, many coming with Luman Shurtliff, who wrote:

"We arrived in Garden Grove, November 15, 1846. In 30 days we had accomplished a journey of 340 miles without means, except the Lord had furnished almost without exertion on our part. Our teams looked well and the teamsters had no sickness and the sick we brought were on the gain except one sister who died soon after we arrived."[38]

The phrase "the Lord had furnished almost without exertion" may refer to the "Miracle of the Quail." On October 9, for whatever logical, natural, or divine reason, flocks of quail descended on the wagon train carrying the

"poor saints." Thomas Bullock recorded, "Some fell on the wagons, some under, some on the breakfast tables. The boys and brethren ran about after them and caught them alive with their hands. . . . Every man, woman and child had quails to eat for their dinner and after dinner the flocks increased in size. . . . This was repeated more than half a dozen times."[39]

Some refugees, like young Joseph Fish and his family, did not travel to the Missouri River but perilously remained behind. He wrote:

"Before we left this camp, my father returned to Nauvoo for the purpose of selling his property. He managed to sell the house and lot for a mere trifle and was glad to get anything he could. He said that there was eleven ball holes through the door, which was probably done by the mob when they entered the city as they pillaged nearly every house and shot into many of them. . . . We were enabled to move on a short distance . . . to the Des Moines River . . .

about four miles below Farmington. Here we spent the winter of 1846–1847. . . . We were told several times during the winter, that we were to be driven out, and we lived in constant fear of being mobbed. . . . On one occasion, my mother went on a friendly visit to the minister's family and told his wife that we had been threatened by the mob and if we were driven out we would come to their place for refuge as she knew that we would be protected by such Christian people. My mother always thought that this made some impression upon the family . . . [as] the minister was counted as one of their number in all these persecutions."[40]

Most, however, did make the journey across Iowa. With so many insisting they not be left behind, along with the growing numbers of sick and destitute, a shortage of provisions and the unanticipated delays while crossing Iowa finally convinced Brigham Young that they would have to winter at the Missouri River. It became apparent that his goal of reaching the Rocky Mountains in 1846 could not be realized.

The American government's request for five hundred Mormon volunteers to serve in the U.S. military in the war against Mexico sealed the decision to winter at the Missouri River. In exchange for raising the needed volunteers for the Mormon Battalion, Brigham Young obtained a concession from Captain James Allen, General Kearney's representative, that the Saints could winter unmolested on lands that belonged to the Indians on both sides of the river.

Getting five hundred men to volunteer for the Mormon Battalion proved a hard sell. Most felt the federal government had done precious little to protect their rights, property, and lives. Now they were being asked to contribute five hundred men to a war effort at a time when these men would be needed to prepare for the Church's move to the far west.

Henry Bigler reflected the feelings of many Church members: "It was against my feelings and against the feelings of my brethren although we were willing to obey counsel believing all things would work for the best in the end. Still it looked hard when we called to mind the mobbings and drivings, the killing of our leaders, the burning of our homes and forcing us to leave the States and Uncle Sam take no notice of it and then to call on us to help fight his battles to me it was an insult."[41]

Brigham Young countered the hard feelings about the military request, marshaling all the arguments he could:

"This is no hoax. Elder Little . . . has been to see the president [of the United States] on the subject of emigrating the saints to the western coast, and confirms all that Captain Allen has stated to us. *The United States want our friendship, the president wants to do us good and secure our confidence.* The outfit of this five hundred men costs us nothing and their pay will be sufficient to take their families over the mountains. There is war between Mexico and the United States, to whom California must fall a prey, and if we are the first settlers, the old citizens cannot have a Hancock or Missouri pretext to mob the saints. *The thing is from above, for our good, has long been understood between us and the United States government. . . . The church could not help the twelve over the mountains, when they wanted to go, and now we will help the churches.*"[42]

Either by the logic of his arguments or the sheer force

of his personality, Brigham Young's efforts had the desired effect. James S. Brown wrote, "Surprised as we were at the government's demand, we were still more so to think our leaders would entertain for a moment the idea of compliance therewith."[43] At a reunion of the Battalion in 1855, he was even more direct, "I do not suppose there is an individual in the battalion, who, had he been left to his own thoughts and feelings, independent of counsel, would have enlisted. I would have felt very reluctant under the circumstances had it not been for the counsel of my brethren who God authorized to dictate the affairs of His kingdom."[44]

Zadoc Judd later wrote about his decision to enlist as an eighteen-year-old:

"This was quite a hard pill to swallow—to leave wives and children on the wild prairie, destitute and almost helpless, having nothing to rely on only the kindness of neighbors, and go to fight the battles of a government that had allowed some of its citizens to drive us from our homes, but the word came from the right source and seemed to bring the spirit of conviction of its truth with it and there was quite a number of [our] company volunteered, myself and brother among them."[45]

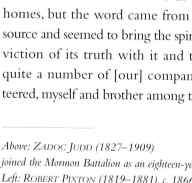

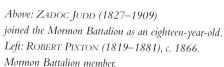

Above: ZADOC JUDD (1827–1909)
joined the Mormon Battalion as an eighteen-year-old.
Left: ROBERT PIXTON (1819–1881), *c. 1866.*
Mormon Battalion member.

It took almost a month, but the Battalion finally attained the full complement of five hundred. With William Pitt's Brass Band providing music, a grand farewell ball was held at the recently constructed bowery on the evening of July 18. On July 20, the Mormon Battalion marched out of the new Mormon settlement of Kanesville toward Fort Leavenworth. Their trek from the banks of the Missouri River to the Pacific Ocean at San Diego would mark one of the longest military marches in American history. After their discharge, many Mormon Battalion veterans would continue to make history, participating in the discovery of California gold and establishing new trails that would be used by the tidal wave of gold-seekers, who in just three years would be racing across the continent for their share of the glittering metal.

The loss of the Battalion was keenly felt by those left behind. In November, Norton Jacob wrote:

"The whole Camp of Winter Quarters was divided into two Bishoprics under the direction of the High Council for the purpose of taking care of the poor, which included the wives of those men who volunteered and went into the army last July."[46]

In addition to the needs of hundreds of Battalion families, the number of poor and destitute Saints swelled as latecomers finished crossing Iowa. The thousands who had arrived formed new settlements, perhaps as many as ninety on the Iowa side of the Missouri River, with Kanesville, later renamed Council Bluffs, becoming the most noted. It even boasted a newspaper run by Apostle Orson Hyde, the *Frontier Guardian*. The Mormons also built the town of Winter Quarters, which served as the Church's

Mormon Battalion Ball, July 1846, *C.C.A. Christensen.*
*At Kanesville the Saints put on a festive dance
for the departing Battalion members.*

headquarters on the river's west side, where a large stock-ade and about seven hundred rudimentary homes were in use by Christmas.

Some of the refugees died before they saw another Christmas. The physical toll exacted crossing Iowa, the desperate lack of provisions, poor living conditions, and another harsh winter proved fatal for hundreds of the Saints. In very personal terms, Lucy Meserve Smith later recalled that winter's miserable circumstances:

"We moved down to Winter Quarters when my babe was two weeks old. There we lived in a cloth tent untill December, then we moved into a log cabin, ten feet square, with sod roof, chimney and only the soft ground for a floor and poor worn cattle beef and corn cracked on a hand mill, for our food. Here I got scurvy, not having any vegetables to eat. I got so low I had to wean my baby and he had to be fed on that coarse cracked corn bread when he was only five months old. We had no milk for a while till we could send to the herd and then he did very well till I got better. My husband took me in his arms and held me till my bed was made nearly every day for nine weeks. I could not move an inch. Then on the 9th of February I was

30 years old. I had nothing to eat but a little corn meal gruel. I told the folks I would remember my birthday dinner when I was 30 years old. My dear baby used to cry till It seemed as tho I would jump off my bed when it came night. I would get so nervous, but I could not even speak to him. I was so helpless I could not move myself in bed or speak out loud. . . . When I got better I had not a morsel in the house I could eat, as my mouth was so sore. . . . Then my companion would take a plate and go around among the neighbors and find some one cooking maybe a calf's pluck. He would beg a bit to keep me from starving. I would taste it and then I would say oh do feed my baby. My appetite would leave me when I would think of my dear child. My stomach was hardening from the want of food.

"The next July my darling boy took sick and on the 22nd, the same day that his father and Orson Pratt came into the valley of the great Salt Lake my only child died. I felt so overcome in my feelings. I was afraid I would lose my mind, as I had not fully recovered from my sickness the previous winter."[47]

Margaret Phelps, whose husband died marching with the Mormon Battalion, wrote of similar privations:

"Winter found me bed-ridden, destitute, in a wretched hovel which was built upon a hillside; the season was one of constant rain; the situation of the hovel and its openness, gave free access to piercing winds and water flowed over the dirt floor, converting it into mud two or three inches deep; no wood but what my little ones picked

ORSON HYDE (1805–1878). Early convert, apostle, and Utah colonizer, c. 1853. Photographer: Marsena Cannon.

Above: WINTER QUARTERS, *C.C.A. Christensen.*
Right: PLAN OF WINTER QUARTERS, *c. 1846. Lots and street names, fall of 1846.*

up around the fences, so green it filled the room with smoke; the rain dropping and wetting the bed which I was powerless to leave."[48]

Such suffering could not continue; the Missouri River settlements were only intended to be temporary, until the Church was ready to move west. In the spring of 1847, Brigham Young left Winter Quarters, leading a hand-picked vanguard company to the Salt Lake Valley. Thousands followed close behind. Yet thousands more remained, and the Winter Quarters–Council Bluffs region became their home for another five years.

Initially, Church leaders did not want all the members to come to the Salt Lake Valley, as there were no means to support them. Later, many of the members in the Winter Quarters area could not afford to emigrate, particularly after the discovery of gold in California dramatically increased the demand and price for teams and wagons. As months turned into years, many Latter-day Saints simply grew comfortable with the area and lost their desire to emigrate west.

It took a direct appeal from the presidency of the Church in 1851 before many would leave for the Salt Lake Valley. Whether reluctantly or willingly, at least ten thousand heeded the call and started out on the trail in the spring and summer of 1852, effectively ending the Mormon presence in western Iowa and Winter Quarters. For those traveling in 1852 as well as those who left before and after them, it remained to be seen whether this next segment of the Mormon Trail held out more hope for the future than the one they followed across Iowa in 1846. ✳

MISHAPS

Guns, Snakes, and Wagons

~~~~~~~~

TRAVELING WESTWARD by wagon train was filled with dangers, some anticipated, others unforeseen. The greatest dangers were disease and mishaps. The most prevalent accidents were shootings (sometimes self-inflicted), drownings, being run over by wagon wheels, and bodily injury from working with livestock.[49] But there were also stampedes, exposure, lightning, hail, ticks, mosquitoes, fatigue, rattlesnakes, bad water, lack of food, and injury during buffalo hunts. Although most pioneers escaped mishaps with only minor scrapes and bruises, accidents sometimes resulted in injuries that crippled or mortally wounded the victim.

Westward travelers were usually well armed even if they lacked adequate experience in handling their weaponry. Abner Blackburn wrote about this experience in the winter of 1846 at Sugar Creek, Iowa: "Met with a severe accident. There was a young gawky fellow fooling with one of those old Flint-Lock horse pistols. It was loaded with three rifle balls. At the discharge of the pistol two of the balls passed through my thigh and one struck the bone. . . . They expected me to pass in my check. Brigham and Kimball were there and prayed me out of danger. My parents came . . . and by good nursing [I] came out as good as new in about six weeks."[50]

The 1856 Daniel McArthur company saw the injury

of two English companions in separate but related incidents. A large rattlesnake bit Mary Bathgate "just above the ankle, on the back part of her leg. She was about a half a mile ahead of the camp at the time it happened. . . . She was generally accompanied by Sister Isabella Park. They were both . . . over 60 years of age, and neither of them had ridden one inch, since they had left the Iowa camp ground. . . . As soon as we heard the news, we left all things. . . . When we got to her, she was quite sick. . . . So we took a pocket knife and cut the wound larger, squeezed out all the bad blood we could. . . . We then took and anointed her leg and head, and laid our hands on her in the name of Jesus and felt to rebuke the influence of the poison. . . . We then told her that she must get into the wagon. . . . We started on and traveled about two miles, when we stopped to take some refreshments. . . . As the word was given for the teams to start, old Sister Isabella Park ran in before the wagon to see how her companion was. The driver, not seeing her, hallooed at his team. . . . Sister Park could not get out of the way, and the fore wheel struck her and threw her down and passed over both her hips. Brother Leonard grabbed hold of her to pull her out of the way, before the wheel could catch her. He only got her out part way and the hind wheels passed over her ankles. We all thought that she would be all mashed to pieces, but to the joy of us all,

LIGHTNING STORM, *William H. Jackson.*

there was not a bone broken, although the wagon had something like two tons burden on it. . . . Although quite sore for a few days, Sister Park got better, so that she was on the tramp before we got into this Valley, and Sister Bathgate was right by her side, to cheer her up."[51]

FLEEING TO ZION

ON APRIL 6, 1847, the seventeenth anniversary of the founding of the Church, Norton Jacob recorded, "A special conference was held in Winter Quarters, Brother John Smith presiding. Brother Brigham addressed the congregation a short time, said that on the morrow he intended to start on his journey west, then proposed that [the] conference proceed to do its business."[1]

The following day Jacob wrote, "About noon I left my family and started on the great expedition with the pioneers to the West. President B. Young and his teams started at the same time. We also had the cannon along, a 6-pounder. We traveled about 10 miles on the divide up the river and camped about sunset near a small grove in a hollow, where we were somewhat shielded from the north wind which was very cold."[2]

After a short, ten-mile start, this first pioneer company halted for several days. Word reached Brigham Young that Apostles Parley P. Pratt and John Taylor had just returned from their mission in England, and Young wanted to meet with them. Taylor brought a number of scientific instruments from England to enable apostle and mathematician Orson Pratt to determine longitude, latitude, elevation, and weather conditions during the journey.

Brigham Young planned as carefully as he could for the trip west by studying the latest maps, reviewing the official reports of Fremont, even consulting Lansford W. Hastings's *The Emigrant's Guide to Oregon and California*. In February 1847 he wrote to Joseph A. Stratton, who presided over the Saints in St. Louis, asking him, "Bring me one half dozen of Mitchell's new map of Texas, Oregon, and California and the regions adjoining, or his accompaniment for the same for 1846, or rather the latest edition and best map of all the Indian countries in North America. . . . If there is anything later or better than Mitchell's, I want the best."[3]

Not only did Brigham want the latest and best information about the route west, but he also carefully chose 144 men to fill the roster of the first pioneer company. No one missed the symbolism of choosing twelve men to represent each of the twelve tribes of Israel. After all, they were the Camp of Israel. However, the final composition of the company differed somewhat from an exact 144. Norton Jacob noted they were "called together by the sound of the bugle at 8 o'clock, when upon numbering there [were] found to be 143 men, 3 women, and 2 children."[4] One man, Ellis Ames, became ill and did not travel, and the three women, Clarissa Decker Young, Ellen Sanders Kimball, and Harriet Young, and the two children, Isaac and Lorenzo Young, accompanied the train at the last minute.

While it was an honor to be a member of this first Mormon pioneer company, it was also a sacrifice few wished to make. Sylvester Earl wrote, "It was hard for me to leave my little family sick among howling wolves and the roaming savages of the West but the servants of the Lord said go and I felt as ever to leave all for the benefit of the Gospel or the salvation of the people."[5]

The circumstances surround-

1846 Mitchell map of western United States. Brigham Young ordered six copies of this map.
Inset: John Taylor (1808–1887).

ing the departure of George A. Smith were particularly difficult. He wrote:

"April 14th [1847]

"I took leave of my family and started for the camp about 9 A.M. I left my youngest child, Nancy Adelia, with inflamation on the brain. It was the opinion of most that she would live but a few hours. Two others of my family were sick. There was enough corn meal to last my family three days and no other provisions. My father let me have a yoke of cattle, rather poor and not well matched, to help me on."[6]

Considering the circumstances, it is surprising he wrote at all. Without a deep and assuring faith, George A. could never have been able to leave a family in such conditions. Undoubtedly to him this was but one more chapter in the trial of his faith, a process that he fully expected would last until the end of his life. Similar heart-rending departures faced many in this first pioneer company now assembling for the journey west.

At last, on April 16, one of the most atypical wagon companies ever to cross the plains began its long trek toward a still undetermined location in the West. After traveling for five cold and dreary days, the company encountered a band of Pawnees. Appleton Harmon wrote, "Arose in the morning as usual at the blast of the winding horn. got up our teams & started on our way and crossed the Looking glass crick about one mile from whare we ware camped and travled about 3 miles when we seen a lone indian approaching toward us from narrow skirt of timber. . . . Soon after several more Indians immerged from the same wood & on coming up to us seemed to extend the hand of fellowship & say how de do."[7]

Levi Jackman further reported, "We had got in a few miles of the Pawnee Indian winter quarters and some few came and met us and seamed verrey friendley. a little after noon we stopt to bait opposite there Camps which was on the outher side of the Loup fork. The Chief and about 30 outhers soon geathered in. they ware friendley and wanted presants. and when we did not give them as mutch Powder [and] tobaco &c as they wanted they ware dissatisfied and the chief would not shake hands with Br Young when they went away."[8]

Howard Egan even said, "They . . . told us we must go back. We paid no attention to them."[9] The company began the difficult crossing of Loup Fork on April 23. The last wagon did not make it across until the afternoon of

Far left: Norton Jacob (1804–1879).
Left: First pioneer women of Utah. *These three women were members of the first wagon company to enter the Salt Lake Valley in July 1847 (left to right):* Ellen S. Kimball (1824–1871), Harriet Page Decker Young (1803–1871), *and* Clarissa Decker Young (1828–1889).

the next day. Their troubles continued when Indians began a sporadic harassment of the company. In the excitement, a horse was accidently shot, which, according to Howard Egan made "four of the best horses in the camp lost in the last four days."[10]

They spent the sabbath, April 25, camped beside Loup Fork. Thomas Bullock related that the Sabbath was observed "as a day of rest, for meditation, prayer & praise." He wrote, "All was harmony, peace, & love. . . . The brethren were called together to worship the Supreme, when Prest. Young called on the Choir to sing 'This land was once a garden place' followed by H.C. Kimball making prayer to our Heavenly Father; several of the brethren then spoke their feelings, & while G. A. Smith was relating the Prophet Joseph's instructions, not to kill any of the animals or birds, or anything created by Almighty God that had life, for the sake of destroying it."[11]

After some consultation, the company made perhaps their most significant decision to that point, electing to travel along the north side of the Platte River. Before this Mormon "vanguard" company, most travelers following the Platte used the south side of the river, as it was generally believed to have better feed.

The vanguard company encountered Charles Beaumont, a member of a small trading company traveling east on the south side of the Platte, who crossed the river on May 4 for a visit. His favorable description of the south side of the Platte caused the company to consider crossing over, but the decision was made to stay on the north side so the subsequent 1847 Mormon companies would be able to follow the track of the vanguard company.

THE PIONEERS.

THE PIONEERS. *Illustration from Stenhouse,* Rocky Mountain Saints.

Egan reported that before Beaumont left, "He agreed to carry letters for us to the settlements. . . . We gave the man some bread and bacon to last him to the settlements. He said he had not eaten any bread for a long time."[12]

The vanguard company's decision to remain on the north side established a pattern for subsequent Mormon companies, which became so firmly entrenched that even non-Mormons called the north side the "Mormon route." Although many Mormons traveled the south side and thousands of non-Mormons throughout the overland emigration period chose the north side, the identification of the north side of the Platte as the "Mormon route" never disappeared.[13]

During the first week of May the company began to encounter buffalo and could not overcome the temptation to hunt. As they continued traveling on the north side of the Platte, the pioneers were astonished at the seemingly endless herds. Appleton Harmon wrote, "Whare we halted the buffalo Seemed to form a complete line from the river, their watering place, [a?] solid column to the Bluffs or on to the bluffs as far as I could Se[e], which was at least 4 mi. they Stood their ground, apparently *amazed at us* until within 30 rods of the waggons when their line was broken by Some taking fright & runing off. others, to satisfy their curiosity, came closer within gun Shot of the camp, Sniffing & Shaking their Shaggy heads, but being pursued by the dogs, runoff.

"At this time I could stand on my wagon and see more than ten thousand buffalo. This was possible because the plain was perfectly black with them on both sides of the river and on the bluff, on our right."[14]

As the month of May wore on, the company approached the confluence of the North and South Platte Rivers. Since they began the trip, members had estimated the mileage covered at the end of each day. This inexact method of gauging mileage caused some argument and was a source of irritation to William Clayton.

Clayton, a stickler for detail, determined that 360 revolutions of Heber C. Kimball's wagon wheel made a mile.

Above: APPLETON MILO HARMON (1820–1877). Pioneer of 1847.
Opposite: APPLETON MILO HARMON DIARY, 1847.

He then tied a red rag to the wheel and counted the revolutions—*all day*—while walking beside the wagon to determine an accurate mileage. This ritual continued for several days when the tedium finally proved too much even for the disciplined Clayton. Soon a primitive odometer was constructed and attached to the wagon. After being attached and used first on the morning of May 12, 1847, it continued in use the rest of their journey to the Salt Lake Valley. Clayton later used the recorded mileage in producing his famous *Latter-Day Saints' Emigrants' Guide.*

Clayton's journal entries describe the installation of the device:

"Tuesday, 11th [May 1847]. . . . Brother Appleton Harmon is working at the machinery for the wagon to tell the distance we travel and expects to have it in operation tomorrow, which will save me the trouble of counting, as I have done, during the last four days. . . ."

"Wednesday, 12th. Morning cool, weather fine. Brother Appleton Harmon has completed the machinery on the wagon so far that I shall only have to count the number of miles, instead of the revolution of the wagon wheel. . . .

"Sunday, 16th. . . . About noon today Brother Appleton Harmon completed the machinery on the wagon called a 'roadometer' by adding a wheel to revolve once in ten miles, showing each mile and also each quarter mile we travel, and then casing the whole over so as to secure it from the weather."[15]

Clayton may have missed much in those few days of meticulously watching the revolving red rag on the wagon

Continued on page 59

After one hours refresh ment we moved on
again 4¾ ms & halted for dinner at ½
past 1 P.M. we got upour teams again & started
at 3 P.M. & traveled 4¾ ms over a wet
bottom owing to the late heavey rains
& camped in a circle
probably 1¼ ms from the river, we got
good water by digging some wells our com-
-ree has been, of, 1,00 our fuel is principle ly
pitch pine that has drifted on shore a long
the river, Chimney rock is in full
view off us & is as rer tinned to be 3 ms in
an air line S. W. by Profesor Pratte
from the camp he all so by his in strumen-
ts found it to be 2 60 feet high
2 antilope killed halted 10 mi to 6 P.M.

Chimney
Rock 260
feet high

Wednesday the 26th fine warm morning
we got upour teams & started at 8 o.M. &
traveled 4½ ms when we ware exactly north
of chimney rock & 3 ms distant we halted
for dinner at 12 m. having traveled
7¼ ms we started again at 25 pas 2 P.M. &
traveled 5 ms & camped in a circle by the river at 5 P.M. 4 antilope killed to day &
destributed through the camp, a tall range
of bluffs extends a long the opposite side the
river which a pears veery broken on
which there is some shrubby cedars, on
guard the fore part of the night, shower
ry this eve ning no buffalo been seen
for several days, a small hunt ing party of
this evening before noon of hostile In-
people the plain, Col markan le pendant
the Col was honorablby a quitted

on
Thursday the 27th a fine morning
the future prospect pleases & nothing to
mar the pease that universally prevails
we got upour teams & started at 5 A.M. &
traveled over a flat level bottom in a stre-
ight line N. W. 8 ms & halted near the
river, & near of a little below Scotts
bluffs that is on the South side the rive at
12 M. for dinner 3 antilope killed & brought to
camp

we started again at 2 P.M. & traveled 5¾ ms
in a N. W. direction & camped in a bend of the
river neard ¼ a mile from the same in
a circle at a qto 5 P.M. having passed Scotts
bluffs a bout 3 ms the river takes a bend of to
the North or nearly so, 1 antilope killed
a heaven North wind, in the evening, feed good, road fair

SCOTT,S

BLUFF,S

A view of a part of the termonation of Scotts
bluffs 2½ ms N E East is where the view was
taken from, this bluff is supposed to be nearly
800 feet above the level of the river, the majority of these bluffs are composed of a kind
of yellow clay, a part of which is conso elated in
to a kind of soft rock, chimney rock is composed of the same materials

1 mile back of us

Above: INDEPENDENCE ROCK, *William H. Jackson. Pioneers looked forward to this landmark, which was named by a party of trappers who stopped here on July 4.*
Opposite: MITCHELL PASS, *William H. Jackson.*

Continued from page 54

wheel. The pioneers encountered a feast of sights, sounds, and scenery as they moved westward. May 20, near Ash Hollow, Appleton Harmon noted that "4 of the Brethering [brethren] . . . crosed the river to ascertain the facts of the oregon trail," and on May 22 he noted, "An Indian boy Came to us last evening but he is verry wild & Shy & has traveld with us to day."[16] The same day Harmon mentioned, "Several petrified bones of enormous sise have been found yesterday & to day which are supposed to be mammoth bones. Several of the brethering [brethren] have visited the bluffs this evening. G[e]orge R. Grant & Orson K. Whitney found & caught a young grey Eagle and brought it to camp. A great miney rattle Snakes of the large kind have been seen with[in] a few days past."[17]

As Harmon's journal entries indicate, the strict regimen of the march began to weaken as one day rolled into the next and as members' early fears of the unknown began to fade. The company of relatively young men, most under the age of forty, began to focus much of their attention on buffalo hunting, playing cards and checkers, wrestling, and playing practical jokes. However, Brigham Young's stern New England sensibilities chaffed at these daily antics. He, more than the others, understood that this was the advance company of the host of Israel fleeing Babylon for the safety of the West. He firmly believed that fact should govern the behavior of the camp, for they were on a sacred mission to save a people, not on a leisurely pleasure trip in the country.

Chimney Rock, *George M. Ottinger.*

Like many western travelers, some members of the camp became obsessed with hunting buffalo. John Brown noted, "There was so much game killed and wasted, that President Young called us together and gave us a little reproof. He said, 'The spirit manifested would soon kill and waste all the game on the plains. Learn to do right without having some one to keep us in remembrance of our duty by reproofs, etc.'"[18] Howard Egan wrote of the same incident, "At 7 o'clock President Young called the Captains of Tens together and gave them instructions not to let their men kill any more game, as we had more on hand now than we could take care of, and for them not to take life merely to gratify their propensities. He also stated that life was as dear to the animal, according to their understanding, as it was to us. That if the horsemen hunters would go ahead and hunt out the road they would be of more utility to the camp than pursuing every band of antelope that passed the camp; that there were men among us in responsible positions who cared no more for the interest of the camp than the horses that they rode; that the spirit of the hunter as was now manifested would lead them to kill all the game within a thousand miles as inconsistently as the butcher would apply the knife to the throat of a bullock."[19]

Finally, on May 29, after several days of unheeded council, Brigham's simmering temper boiled over. In the morning, after the bugle call, he held a meeting of the

entire camp. In a heated address he stated his position in terms that were unmistakable: "Give me the man of prayer; give me the man of faith; give me the man of discretion; a sober-minded man, and I would rather go among the savages with six or eight such men, than to trust myself with the whole of this camp with the spirit they now possess. . . . We suppose that we are going to look out a home for the Saints, a resting place, a place of peace, where we can build up the Kingdom and bid the nations welcome, without a low, mean, dirty, trifling, covetous, wicked spirit dwelling in our bosoms. . . . I am one of the last to ask my brethren to enter into a solemn covenant, but, if they will not enter into a solemn covenant to put away their iniquity, and turn to the Lord, and serve Him, and acknowledge and honor His name, I want them to take their wagons and return back, FOR I SHALL NOT GO ANY FARTHER under this state of things. If we don't repent and quit our wickedness, we will have more hinderances than we have had and worse storms to encounter."[20]

Brigham's reproach had the desired effect. William Clayton recorded:

"Being half past one o'clock we again pursued our journey in peace, all reflecting on what has passed today, and many expressing their gratitude for what has transpired. It seemed as though we were just commencing on this important mission, and all realizing the responsibility resting upon us to conduct ourselves in such a manner that the journey may be an everlasting blessing to us,

Opposite: WHITE MEN KILLING BUFFALO, *William H. Jackson.*
Right: HOWARD EGAN (1815–1878), *pioneer and frontiersman, c. 1868.*

instead of an everlasting disgrace. No loud laughter was heard, no swearing, no profane language, no hard speeches to man or beast, and it truly seemed as though the cloud had burst and we had emerged into a new element, a new atmosphere, and a new society."[21]

Five days later, Brigham sent Apostle Amasa Lyman back along the trail to help guide the sick detachment of the Mormon Battalion and the rest of the Mississippi Saints. When Amasa found the group, he reproved them as Brigham had done with the vanguard company. Battalion member John Steele wrote, "Amas E. Lyman preached and said he had watched us and to leave off our folly and be men of God."[22] Abner Blackburn recalled the mixed results:

"Some were in the shade reading novels [and] another the bible, some mending clothes, others shoeing cattle and a number in a tent playing the violin. By and by a runner come around to notify the company that our minister was a going [to] observe the sabbath and preach a sermon. All hands quit work and the fiddle stopt playing. They went into [a] tent to play cards. A few took their guns and went hunting and a few heard the sermon. Such is life on the plains."[23]

One of the problems Amasa faced was a potential mutiny by the sick detachment. Some of these Battalion members spent a miserable winter in Pueblo, had been away from their families for almost a year, and wanted to return to Winter Quarters. In a letter to

Left: AMASA LYMAN (1813–1877), Mormon apostle.

Brigham Young on June 28, Amasa related his efforts to change attitudes among the disaffected Battalion members. In a meeting before the entire sick detachment, he "laid before them the instructions from the council which had the effect to quell the Spirit of mutiny that was among them & instead [of] leaving at F.T. [Fort] John [Laramie] as they had calculated they concluded to follow the counsel & a good spirit had prevailed since in the camp."[24]

The vanguard company came in sight of Fort Laramie on June 1. As a major resting and reprovisioning point for almost all emigrants on the trek west, it was a welcome sight. John Brown noted that waiting for the company was "Brother Crow from Pueblo with six wagons. He had been here two weeks waiting for the first company of Saints to come on. . . . The remainder of the company at Pueblo were waiting to come with a detachment of the Battalion that wintered there."[25]

Norton Jacob's record of meeting the Mississippi Saints revealed that, like the Saints in Winter Quarters, they had suffered privations, and some had died:

"There was a Brother Crow at the Fort, who met our advance guard at the river, having discovered us with a glass from the tower of the Fort when we were some distance below. He was much rejoiced to meet us. He went up with the Mississippi company last summer to Fort Pueblo, 250 miles south of here, and wintered there. Brother Crow, his two sons-in-law, with their families, have been here 2 weeks anxiously waiting for some of the Saints to come up, and had heard nothing definite about our movements. They were 15 days on their journey, and

Continued on page 65

NATIVE AMERICANS

MORMONS and Native Americans interacted throughout the twenty-two years that the Mormon Trail carried emigrants to the Salt Lake Valley. Hostilities rarely erupted; for the most part, their relationship was one of amicable trading, curiosity, and sometimes mutual admiration. Difficulties generally revolved around theft of stock, toll demands by Indians, and cultural misunderstandings about the concept of property ownership.

Instances of conflict occurred in 1848 when Jacob Weatherby was killed returning to Winter Quarters, and Howard Egan, Thomas Ricks, and William Kimball were wounded at the Elkhorn trying to recover stolen cattle. Almon Babbitt and his small party were wiped out while returning east on the trail in 1856. James G. Bleak, who passed the site of the attack, later saw "some Soldiers out Indian hunting."[26] As the years passed and Native Americans felt increasingly pressed by the massive tide of emigration, the level of tension increased. Understandably, as the Indians lost more, they began to demand more.

The Levi Hammon Emigrating Company journal noted that the company was delayed by Indians who refused to allow them to cross the Elkhorn, and Mary Jane Bethers York recalled that her father gave some Sioux a dog for the privilege of allowing her family to cross the Loup Fork bridge.[27] James Henry Rollins wrote that near Laramie, Indians squatted on the trail demanding payment for the water and grass the company had used, which they wanted before allowing the Mormons to pass.[28] At Chimney Rock, Diana Eldredge Smoot wrote that the Sioux demanded the emigrants not kill deer or buffalo.[29] In 1865, the only known direct Indian attack on a Mormon train occurred at Cottonwood Hollow beyond Fort Laramie.[30] During the early 1860s, the federal military presence all but disappeared because of the Civil War, and many westbound trains experienced trouble. However, most of the conflicts occurred between Great Basin tribes and non-Mormon trains traveling to Oregon or California beyond Fort Hall.[31]

One potential point of conflict was the different concepts of property ownership that existed between Indians and almost all trail emigrants. Isabella Horne recorded that an Indian offered a pony for her baby. When she refused to make the trade, he gradually raised the offer to four horses. While the men were trading with the emigrants, women and children walked through the train taking whatever articles they thought useful.[32] Indians offered twenty-five horses, beads, jewelry, buffalo robes, and blankets for five-year-old Nancy Mattice and almost succeeded in stealing Nancy's three-month-old stepsister.[33] An Indian offered Appleton Milo Harmon twenty horses for his wife, Elmeda.[34] Indians also sold many articles, including moccasins, to passing emigrants.

Not only did Latter-day Saints note the trading habits of Native Americans, but they also made distinctions between tribes, with the Sioux almost always receiving

ENCAMPMENT ON THE PLATTE RIVER, *Worthington Whittredge.*

admiring remarks in diaries and journals. Mormons also recorded their dealings with Cherokee, Crow, Otoe, Omaha, Pawnee, Ponca, Shoshone, and Snake. Many journal keepers also noticed the talents and customs of the Indians and recorded the interactions of themselves and other emigrants with Native Americans.

John Pulsipher spoke respectfully of the manner in which the Indians killed buffalo, not wasting any of the meat.[35] At Fort Laramie, young Christopher Jacobs was asked by his friends to perform some acrobatics for a large group of Indians who had assembled at the fort. He recalled, "The Indians gathered around and I turned a couple of somersaults. They were amazed. They stood on the ground and jumped up and down on it to see if it would spring with them. Finding that the ground was solid they came and felt of my legs and talked among themselves much surprised that such a thing was possible."[36] The company journal of the George Benjamin Wallace Emigrating Company notes that the Sioux, when they visited the camp, came "singing and dancing." The Mormons, in turn, held a dance to violin, fife, and drummers, and they also fired the cannon for their guests.[37] Hezekiah Mitchell describes coming "in sight of a Sioux Camp of Indians, about 4000 in number." He wrote, "We had to pass right through them, however as we were making headway, we had intelligence that they were our friends [and] as such we turned to the right and camped amongst them." Mitchell and his wife watched the Sioux dance, sing, and play music inside "a large round tent" but "did not like their ways" and soon left.[38]

Although there were some difficulties, Mormon encounters with Native Americans were generally friendly, and sometimes helpful, as in the experience of John Parry, an 1856 handcart pioneer who wrote, "Indians met us sometimes, and helped us pull our carts which was a great fun for them."[39] Similar entries can be found in the pages of many Mormon pioneer journals. Faithful Mormon journal writers have left an important record of the Native Americans' efforts to survive the unsympathetic and hostile tide of westward immigration that swept across their lands.

Continued from page 62

report that the detachment of our soldiers at that place are preparing to come on and join us, together with the other brethren that are there. Four have died."[40]

Wilford Woodruff also recorded details of the encounter with the Mississippi Saints not included in the journals of Brown and Jacob:

"Camped on the bank of the platt opposite of Fort Laramie within 1 1/2 miles of the fort. When we arived we saw some men Approaching us from the fort. When they arived on the bank we found them to be a part of the company of the Mississippi Brethren who had been to Pueblo through the winter. Brother Crow & his family 7 waggons & 14 souls were the individuals who were at the fort. They soon stood upon the bank of the river. We lanchd our boat & crossed the stream to them. . . . Br Crow Came across & met in Council with us, And informed us that the remainder of the Missippi company with the portion of the Mormon Battalion that was at *Pueblo* would start for Laramie About the first of June & follow our trail onto Calafornia."[41]

Some members of the vanguard company crossed the river and took time to view the fort, which Wilford Woodruff described in some detail on June 2, 1847:

"In company with the Twelve & others I

crossed to the river to visit the fort & those who inhabit it. We exhamined for[t] St John which is now evacuated but the walls are standing. The dimentions of St John are 144 by 132 outside. The inside of the fort contained 16 rooms, 7 rooms on the North west & 7 on the South east one on the South, the largest on the north 98 feet long 47 wide. The Oregon trail runs one rod from the S.W. cornor of the fort. We next visited Fort Larimie now occupied by 38 persons French mostly, who have Married the Sioux. Mr Burdow is the superinteder. This fort is 168 by 116 outside. Thire are 6 rooms upon two sides, & 3 rooms upon the north & 3 upon the south occupied by stores Blacksmith & dwellings. It is quite A plesant situation for A fort."[42]

Appleton Harmon also noted the visit to the fort, even sketching it. He also commented on the information Bordeaux provided about the trail ahead:

"We went in to the Fort & was kindly & genteely received by Mister Bordeaux, the maniger or master of the Fort. he invited us into a room up Stairs which look verry mutch like a bar room of an eastern hotel. it was ornamented with Several drawings, portraits, &c. a long desk, a settee, & some chairs constituted the principal furniture of the room. it was neat & comfortable. Mr. Bordeaux answered the miney questions that was asked him by us a bout the country & the Natives, &c. he sed the seasons ware ginerally dry; that thare had been no rain for 2 years until within a fiew days. he said that the Sioux would not disturb the emegrants but the Crows ware verry annoy[ing]. . . . He expected Some oregon emegrants Soon. he Said that the next fort or trading post we came to was fort Bridger, the other side [of] the mountains. . . . We went through the fort being conducted by Mr. Bordeaux and viewed its ConStruction. I took a

Above: WILFORD WOODRUFF (1807–1898), c. 1853.
This fly-fishing apostle became the third president of the LDS Church.
Photographer: Marsena Cannon.
Right: FORDING THE PLATTE RIVER, 1866.
Photographer: Charles R. Savage.
Far right: MOUNTAIN MAN JIM BRIDGER, *who advised*
Brigham Young not to settle in the Salt Lake Valley.

Sketch of the fort, allso the size, which will be given here-after."[43]

At this point the vanguard company ferried all their wagons to the south side and were now traveling on the Oregon Trail. Soon they rubbed shoulders with other emigrant companies, some from Missouri. Norton Jacob noted, "They came to us and hired Brother Frost to do some blacksmith work for them, having no mechanics with them. Some of them have been engaged with the mobocrats heretofore."[44]

Within two days of leaving Fort Laramie, the company passed two trains of Oregon-bound emigrants and met a party of eastbound traders, who told them about a boat made of buffalo skins concealed at the crossing of the North Fork of the Platte. A detachment, almost a third of the company, was sent ahead to secure the boat and prepare the way for the rest of the company to ferry. They never found the buffalo-skin boat, but they went to work preparing a raft to ferry the company.

When the main company reached the ferry point on June 12, they found the advance group ferrying Oregon emigrants for an agreed-upon price, paid in provisions. The vanguard company remained at the ferry site until June 19. It became readily apparent that the ferry site could serve as a revenue producer for the Church. Wilford Woodruff recorded, "President Young thought it wisdom to leave A number of the brethren here & keep a ferry untill our Company Came up. Emegrants will pay for ferrying $1.50 cts per waggon."[45]

As they traveled through South Pass, they encountered famous mountain man Jim Bridger, who was traveling east from his fort to Fort Laramie. Church leaders spent considerable time mining Bridger's extensive knowledge of the Intermountain West. Wilford Woodruff wrote:

"[Bridger] was expecting us & was to have an interview with President Young & the Twelve And also we wished to have an interview with Him. So we immediately turn onto the creek we nooned on & camped for the night & Mr Bridger & his men Camped with us. We met in Council & spent some hours in conversations. We found him to have been a great traveller And A great knowledge of nearly all Oregon & Calafornia the Mountains, lakes, Rivers, Brooks, springs, valleys mines,

FORT BRIDGER; *Black's Fork of the Green River, Wyoming.*

bring A great population into the bason untill [they] ascertained whether grain would grow or not."[48] Traveling days behind the vanguard company, members of the sick detachment of the Mormon Battalion also encountered Jim Bridger, who was much more blunt about the prospects of agriculture in the Great Basin. Battalion member John Steele recorded, "Captain Brown invited me to go ahead with him to Fort Bridger. We found the old mountaineer and in conversation he told us we could not live in Salt Lake valley for it froze every month in the year and [he] would give us a thousand dollars for the first ear of corn raised there, but if we would give him $1000 he would take us to the G-d-d best valley ever was. I spoke to Captain Brown if it was a G-d-d valley we did not want to go there."[49]

The vanguard company met Sam Brannan on June 30 at the Green River. Brannan, the ecclesiastical leader of the Saints who sailed on the ship *Brooklyn,* had arrived in California in August 1846. In the spring of 1847 he set out to meet the vanguard company and assist them to California. Brigham Young had decided against going as far west as the coast, and despite Brannan's glowing reports of the region bordering the Pacific, the Mormon leader seemed disposed to settle near the Great Salt Lake. Horace K. Whitney gave this account of the meeting:

"During this afternoon we were all much surprised by the unexpected arrival of Elder Samuel Brannan who was at the head of the company of the brethren that went round by sea last year from New York city to California—He was

Creeks, &c if what He told us was true, He knew of gold, silver, copper, lead Coal Iron, Sulpher & Saltpeter mines."[46]

Concerning the Salt Lake Valley, Bridger said "there was but one thing that Could operate against it becoming A great grain country & that wold be frost. He did not know but the frost would effect the corn. . . . We conversed about A great variety of things. He said he was Ashamed of the Maps of Freemont for He knew nothing about the Country, ownly the plain travled road, that He Could Correct all the maps that had been put out about the western world."[47]

As they parted company the next day, Bridger repeated his concern "that it would not be prudent to

accompanied by 3 men, 2 of whom had come thro' with him from the latter country—with 1 of them I was well acquainted. This man is [Charles C.] Smith & is I believe some distant relation of our prophet Joseph. He left Nauvoo (where I made his acquaintance) some 2 years since for Oregon. One of the other 2 men was one of the individuals seen with Mr. Bridger the other day—the other man I did not know. Elder Brannan gives a very favorable account of climate, soil, etc. of California & appears quite anxious that we should immediately go there to take possession of the country before it becomes occupied by others. He had left Yerba Buena April 13th—This place is situated on the bay of San Francisco & from all accounts bids fair to become in time a flourishing city. He brought a number of news papers with him which he distributed among the 'Twelve'—among these was a file of his own entitled the 'California Star' 12 all in number. Mr Smith informed us that in Oregon they had 2 seasons, rust & dry.[50]

Thirteen Mormon Battalion veterans from the sick detachment overtook the company on July 4 and traveled with them. Within three days, the company reached Fort Bridger. Near this famous fort, the Oregon Trail swung north, but the vanguard company would continue a westward track for another one hundred miles to the Salt Lake Valley, often following the faint trail of the Donner Party from the previous year.

They soon approached the Bear River, one of the last river crossings on the Mormon Trail. Near this site mountaineer Miles Goodyear met the vanguard company on July 10 and tried to persuade them to travel north toward his trading post near the mouth of the Weber River.

William Clayton recorded that the Church leaders doubted Goodyear's motives:

"Mr. Miles Goodyear came into camp. . . . We are now within two miles of Bear River. His report of the [Great Salt Lake] valley is more favorable than some we have heard but we have an idea he is anxious to have us make a road to his place through selfish motives. . . . There is scarcely any wagon track to be seen on the northern road, only a few wagons of Hasting's company having come this route; the balance went the other road and many of them perished in the snow."[51]

After crossing the Bear River, the company continued on until they came to some interesting rock formations known as "The Needles," near Yellow Creek, where they halted temporarily because some, including Brigham Young, were becoming ill. William Clayton recorded that during the day, "President Young was taken very sick awhile before we halted. After resting two hours the camp moved on again, except President Young and Kimball's wagons, who concluded to remain there today on account of the President's sickness."[52]

Two days later, Albert Rockwood wrote in his journal that he was suffering from a similar affliction: "Br. Young is a little better. The fever rages harder than ever on me. Br. Lorenzo Young and

Above right: SAM BRANNAN (1819–1889) met Brigham Young in what is now Wyoming and argued for settling in California. Right: HORACE K. WHITNEY (1823–1884), pioneer of 1847, musician, mathematician, and printer.

many others look upon me as dangerously ill. I so considered myself and so told the brethren that if no relief came in the hour, they might dig a hole to put me in. . . . Rested some this night."[53] Some have speculated that the sudden illness that struck many in the camp may have been Rocky Mountain spotted fever, an affliction received from ticks.

On July 13 and for the balance of the journey, the vanguard company was split into three groups, Orson Pratt and an advance party, the main company, and a rear detachment carrying the sick. After crossing the Weber River, the main company entered Echo Canyon on July 16. Clayton recorded his impression of the unusual acoustic and scenic characteristics of the canyon:

"There is a very singular echo in this ravine, the rattling of wagons resembles carpenters hammering at boards inside the highest rocks. The report of a rifle resembles a sharp crack of thunder and echoes from rock to rock for some time. The lowing of cattle and braying of mules seem to be answered beyond the mountains. Music, especially brass instruments, have a very pleasing effect and resemble a person standing inside the rock imitating every note. The echo, the high rocks on the north, high moun-

Above left: ORSON PRATT *(1811–1881), c. 1849.*
Apostle and advance scout into the Salt Lake
Valley for the vanguard wagon company.
Engraver: Frederick Piercy.
Above right: ECHO CANYON, *William H. Jackson.*

tains on the south with the narrow ravine for a road, form a scenery at once romantic and more interesting than I have ever witnessed."[54]

When the Battalion sick detachment reached the canyon days later, Abner Blackburn, with less polish but as much enthusiasm, remarked, "Crosed to Echo Canion, that celebrated place whear every noise makes an echo. The boys made all the noise they could going through. It was truely wonderful."[55]

Finally the company approached the Valley of the Great Salt Lake. Orson Pratt recorded his first view of the valley on July 21:

"No frost this morning but a heavy dew. we resumed our journey, came 2 1/2 miles & assended a mountain for 1 1/2 miles. descended upon the west side 1 mile. came upon a swift running creek where we halted for noon (we called this Last Creek). Bro. Erastus Snow, (having overtook our camp from the other camp which he said were but a few miles in the rear) & myself proceeded in advance of the camp down Last Creek 4 1/2 miles to where it passes through a Kanyon & issues into the broad open valley below. To avoid the Kanyon the waggons last season had passed over an exceedingly steep & dangerous hill. Mr Snow & myself asscended this hill from the top of which a broad open valley about 20 miles wide & 30 long lay stretched out before us at the N. End of which the broad waters of the great Salt Lake glistened in the sunbeams, containing high mountainous Islands from 25 to 30 miles in extent. After issuing from the mountains, among which we had been shut up for many days & beholding in a moment such an extensive scenery open before us we could not refrain from a shout of joy which almost involuntarily escaped from our lips the moment this grand & lovely scenery was within our view. We immediately descended very gradually into the lower parts of the valley & although we had but one horse between us yet we traversed a circuit of about 12 miles before we left the valley to return to our camp, which we found encamped 1 1/2 miles up the ravine from the valley & 3 miles in advance of their noon halt. (it was about 9 o'clock in the evening when we got into camp. The main body of the pioneers who were in the rear were encamped only 1/2 mile up the creek from us with the exception of some waggons containing some who were sick who were still behind."[56]

Contrary to perceptions that the valley was entirely desert, the first Saints encountered something quite different. Often journals from the era describe the valley in terms more positive than negative. Norton Jacob, while noting the region's aridity, wrote of the place, "If it could receive timely rains, it would be one of the most beautiful, fertile regions on the face of the earth; being watered by numerous brooks and rivulets perpetually flowing out of the mountains on every side, filled with trout; which, with the various kinds of rich grass and rushes, renders it one of the best grazing countries that can be found."[57]

Abner Blackburn, commenting on the decision to settle in the Salt Lake Valley, wrote, "They had a buetifel location for a city here, [with] the ice cold watter coming out of canion and spreading over the fertile plains whitch appeard to be rich to the view." Journalist Thomas Bullock recorded that the valley had "wheat grass, which grows six or seven feet high, many different kinds of grasses appear, some being 10 or 12 feet high."[58]

Still, this was not the Midwest by any stretch of the imagination, and contrasting the valley with Missouri or Illinois could easily lead a Mormon pioneer to regard this promised land as barren.[59] Harriet Young exclaimed, "We

ENTERING THE GREAT SALT LAKE VALLEY, *C.C.A. Christensen.*

have traveled fifteen hundred miles to get here, and I would willingly travel a thousand miles farther."[60] Regardless of opinions about its suitability, Church leaders viewed the valley as a gift from God. Wilford Woodruff recorded that it was a "land of promise held in reserve by the hand of GOD for a resting place for the Saints."[61] Brigham Young, traveling sick in Wilford Woodruff's spring carriage, asked Woodruff to stop as they came in sight of the valley. Young recorded, "I directed Elder Woodruff, who had kindly tendered me the use of his carriage, to turn the same half way round, so that I could have a view of a portion of Salt Lake valley. The Spirit of Light rested upon me, and hovered over the valley, and I felt that there the saints would find protection and safety."[62]

Brigham Young entered the valley on the following day, July 24, a day still celebrated by Latter-day Saints as "Pioneer Day." Crops were already being planted, and the waters of City Creek were being diverted for irrigation. The process of settlement began immediately, but within a month many of these original pioneers, including Brigham Young, were now backtracking east to help the emigration from Winter Quarters. As they traveled east, they soon encountered other Latter-day Saints on the trail numbering more than fifteen hundred. The meetings of the westbound Mormons and the eastbound pioneers were filled with rejoicing. The returning pioneers first encountered the Daniel Spencer company. Patty Sessions, a noted Mormon midwife, wrote:

"Saturday 4 [September] go 1 mile stop good feed here the Pioneers came to us it mad[e] our hearts glad to see them they staid all night with us eat and drank with us had a good meeting Sunday 5 they bid us good by with their blessing and left us to go to their families they gave a good report of the valley said it was the place for us."[63]

Later that day, after meeting Parley P. Pratt's westbound company, Thomas Bullock recorded, "The brethren engaged in visiting with P.P. Pratt's Co.—mutually gratified at the opportunity—& such good feelings existed that we did not separate until after 9."[64]

Brigham Young and members of the original pioneer company were not the only ones headed east toward Winter Quarters. William Hyde, traveling with a company of Mormon Battalion vets, recorded, "Reached the camp

of the saints in Salt Lake Valley on the 12th of October. The reception with which we met gladened our hearts and revived our spirits. A small portion of the company found their families here, and consequently had got home. The Presidency and some of the pioneers had returned to Winter Quarters. The saints that were remaining felt very well p[le]ased with the situation of the Valley, and my conclusions were that it was a place of retreat, or a hiding place which God had, in his wisdom, prepared for his people."[65]

Intent on being with their families, Hyde and sixteen others started east on October 16, despite the danger of the late season. Perhaps having survived the deserts of the Southwest in their two-thousand-mile march to San Diego and subsequent trip to northern California, over the Sierra and across the Great Basin, they felt they could handle any trip, in any weather. After a journey that can only be described as difficult, they arrived at Loup Fork on November 28. Hyde described the river as "swolen and so much ice running that it was impossible to get across. . . . We concluded to go up to the forks of the river, which was some 12 or 15 miles distance through brush and over broken ridges without any road or trail. After reaching the forks we were two days before we succeeded in getting all things across."[66]

On December 9 they finally considered giving up. Hyde wrote:

"We camped within about 15 miles of the horn

Patty Sessions (1795–1892), pioneer midwife.

[Elkhorn River], which place is 30 miles from the general camp of the Saints, or Winter Quarters. But as we were strangers to the route, we were not aware that we were so near our place of destination, and as the snow was deep, and our meat which we had saved from the horse entirely exhausted, we seated ourselves upon the snow around our camp fire and entered into council as to the wisest course to be pursued. Some thought best to send two men on two of the best mules in camp for Winter Quarters. To this I replied that we had now traveled near five thousand miles, and that we had suffered much with hunger, cold, thirst and fatigue, and now to give out on the last hundred miles I didn't like the idea. I then said that in case we could not get through with out, we would make a free will offering of my riding mule and we would eat her, as she was in as good order as any in camp. To this proposition all readily agreed.

"On the morning of the 10th, we all were united in calling on the Lord to regard our situation in mercy and send us food from an unexpected quarter that we might have wherewith to subsist upon. And here the Lord heard our prayer. Soon after reaching the Horn, the wild turkeys began to pass our camp in droves, and such a sight I never before witnessed. Drove after drove continued to pass through the woods until night set in. We succeeded in getting four, which was one to every four persons. . . .

"The 11th. Went to the camps of the saints at Winter Quarters. The day was bitter cold and the company was well nigh used up. Our clothing being in no wise calculated for winter, we had suffered much with cold, as well as with hunger. Brother Ira Miles, from poor health and extreme suffering, had become as helpless as a child. But the reception with which we met, and the blessings that were poured upon our heads on our arrival, seemed to cause new life to spring up and to compensate us for all our toils. This company, numbering 16 souls, were the first to return from the Battalion after our discharge in California."[67]

Certainly in 1847 the Mormon Trail had proven to be a "trail of hope." It brought the hoped-for refuge, the hoped-for return of family members, the hoped-for escape from years of persecution. For Patty Sessions the trail provided "the place for us," and for William Hyde, the trail brought the Saints to "a place of retreat, or a hiding place which God had, in his wisdom, prepared for his people." Their thoughts echoed those of thousands of Mormons fleeing west to their new Zion. Hope had been crushed before; would this new trail of hope bring a lasting refuge, or would new trials test them again? For now, it was enough to feel free from the burdens of the past, even if the cost, at times, proved high. ✳

Above: WILLIAM HYDE (1818–1874).
Right: FIRST VIEW OF GREAT SALT LAKE VALLEY FROM BIG MOUNTAIN.

A DAY IN THE LIFE

THE PARTICULARS of daily life varied from company to company over the twenty-two years of Mormon westward migration. However, in April 1847 Brigham Young laid out the ideal "order for travelling and camping" as his religious refugees readied to begin the first massive push toward the Valley of the Great Salt Lake. Diarist William Clayton recorded, "[April 18, 1847] At 5:00 in the morning the bugle is to be sounded as a signal for every man to arise and attend prayers before he leaves his wagon. Then cooking, eating, feeding teams & c. till 7 o'clock at which time the Camp is to move at the sound of the bugle. Each teamster to keep beside his team, with their loaded gun in their hands or in their wagon where they can get them in a moment. The extra men, each to walk opposite his wagon with his loaded gun on his shoulder, and no man to be permitted to leave his wagon unless he obtains permission from his officer. In case of an attack from Indians or hostile appearances the wagons to travel in double file. The order of encampment to be in a circle with the mouth of the wagon to the outside, and the horses and stock tied inside the circle. At 8½ P.M. the bugles to be sounded again at which time all to have prayers in their wagons and to retire to rest by 9 o'clock."[68]

The 1861 recordings of George Teasdale show that after fourteen years of Mormon wagon-train experience, the routine was somewhat modified and streamlined but clearly similar to that of 1847: "August 16th [1861] Sun rises, camp-guard calls up the people and in a short time all are busy cooking breakfast, washing, dressing children and preparing for the days journey. Horn blows for prayers, breakfast is dispatched, the voice of the Cap[tain] is heard 'Oh yes get up the cattle' a general bustle to clear away pack up and get ready to start. The cattle is correlled, yoked up hitched up and out we roll once more at 1/2 past 8. . . . Travel 7 miles correll water the cattle get [the noon] dinner hitch up and off again over a rough road for 8 miles and correll once more get supper and as it is a fine moonlight night got in groups sitting round the fires talking merrily, horn blows we assemble for prayers and instructions are given realative to our duties by Cap. Johnson, interpretated to the Swiss by Bro Woodward the evening hymn and Benediction closes the scene and all retire to rest."[69]

The springless, cushionless wagon seats made wagon riding uncomfortable. Therefore, most pioneers—children and adults—journeyed on foot as the oxen-pulled wagons plodded along at less than two miles per hour. This also reduced the weight of the load. Traveling fifteen miles was considered a very good day—nine was average in the 1840s; but by the 1860s trains could average an amazing twenty miles per day, often twenty-five. By midday both oxen and humans were ready for the "nooning" break. Seventeen-year-old emigrant Margaret Judd [Clawson] fondly remembered, "The best of all meals to me while on our journey was our mid-day luncheon. Mother used to make a kettle of corn meal mush in the morning, then wrapped it up to keep it warm. After the milking was done, the milk was put in a tin churn and wrapped to

THE EMIGRANT TRAIN BEDDING DOWN FOR THE NIGHT,
Benjamin Franklin Reinhart.

keep from slopping it over. When we camped at noon to let the cattle feed, Mother used to bring out the mush and milk. Why, it was too good for poor folks. . . . I never heard of any one complain of a poor appetite while crossing the plains. . . . Bread and bacon were more delicious then than plum pudding or pound cake now. How environments change our tastes."[70]

Although pioneer James Henry Linford remembered "there was a sameness in every day's travel,"[71] the routine could easily be and often was interrupted by mishaps, deaths, occasional (hostile or friendly) visits from Indians and other emigrant parties, bad weather, stampedes, and the

quarrels and misunderstandings that inevitably arose between company members. There were also such diversions as hunting, fishing, and climbing rock formations, and in the evenings there was music, an occasional dance, and storytelling and singing around the campfire. Even Linford admitted that the sameness changed when they "got into the mountains," where ascending long stretches often taxed the stamina of oxen and then descending from mountain passes strained the skills and patience of pioneers.

THE GOLD RUSH

THE YEAR 1848 became the last that the Mormon Trail was a "trail of hope" only for Mormons. The discovery of gold in January 1848 at Sutter's mill in the foothills of California's Sierra Nevada mountains forever altered the character of the Mormon Trail. Beginning with the emigration season of 1849 and continuing for years, the Salt Lake Valley became a temporary resting place for thousands on their way to California who hoped to strike it rich in the gold fields.

The discovery of gold and its potential impact was unknown to the three major Mormon companies emigrating to Salt Lake in 1848. Headed by Brigham Young and apostles Heber C. Kimball and Willard Richards, all of whom had returned to Winter Quarters just weeks after their 1847 arrival in the Salt Lake Valley, these three trains brought an additional 2,400 settlers to the Salt Lake Valley. Like those of the vanguard company the year before, many

of the 1848 emigrants kept journals and diaries, including the richly detailed official account of the Brigham Young company penned by "Church Scribe" Thomas Bullock, who served as Young's clerk.

The accounts of Brigham Young's 1848 company revealed much about the man who would lead the Church for the next three decades. Although often sharp in word, his compassion expressed itself in acts of kindness to company members. During the '48 crossing, Brigham Young set a young boy's broken leg, fixed a family's wagon axletree, and often traveled at the back of the train, breathing the trail dust that every emigrant detested. Richard Ballantyne recorded Brigham's attitude about traveling at the back of the train as well as his metaphor about the locking of wagons at the end of the day:

"Monday . . . 1848 June [25] . . . [Brigham Young] said in regard to travelling behind the Company that he was the Horns of Joseph and was pushing the people together, thereby fulfilling the Scripture. Said in regard to

Opposite: COVERED WAGONS.

Karelling [corralling] that he Knew how nigh a man was to Mormonism by the way he Karelled in the evening. When he Karelled he wanted to lock wheels with his brother so if the Indians should Come upon us or a storm arise the Horses might not be stole nor the waggons upset. Some men wanted to travel with him in the morning, but When evening Came they wanted to Karell about four feet apart so if any danger should arise they might have an opportunity to dodge behind their waggons. He wanted to lock wheels, just as he would lock arms with his brother, so as they might be mutually strengthened."[1]

Not that Brigham Young or any of the Latter-day Saints possessed perfect dispositions or failed to display the frailties of human nature. One faithful soul, Jacob Gates, had a particularly bad day in July as recorded by Oliver Boardman: "Sunday July 9th [1848] was my day to herd cattle which I done all day. We were then 380½ miles from Winter Quarters and had traveled 78 miles the last week. As yet the camp and in fine, all the camps

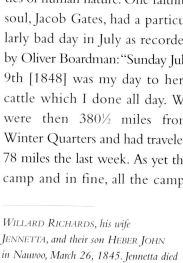

WILLARD RICHARDS, his wife JENNETTA, and their son HEBER JOHN in Nauvoo, March 26, 1845. Jennetta died three and a half months after this daguerreotype was taken. Willard Richards was an apostle and a confidant of Brigham Young. Photographer: Lucian Foster.

had got along well, and with few accidents. Three had been run over in our camp and one wagon turned over which was brother Gates'. He blamed his women severly for it, and what mortified him worse than all, it disclosed a bbl. of wine; before unknown. The wagon turned square bottom side up, no one in it."

Apparently neither Gates nor his wife could put the incident behind them and continued arguing late that night. Boardman recorded, "The guard about 11 o'clock saw it and when the hour came to cry, he loudly cried 11 o'clock, all is well and Gates is quarreling with his wife like hell."[2]

In fairness, Gates's life should not be measured against one bad day.[3] The monotony of travel often made tempers flair. The social discipline of Mormon trains usually prevented companies from splitting up completely. Companies splitting up and joining other trains occurred with regularity among non-Mormon companies, where reasons other than religion were the motivation to travel west. Also, the 1848 emigration was a fraction of what it would be in the next two years, helping to minimize the difficulties that tended to split up traveling companies.

While the '48 emigration trains prepared to travel the Mormon Trail, another amazing odyssey was about to begin more than two thousand miles away, on the west slopes of California's Sierra Nevada mountains. In the summer of 1848, many former Mormon Battalion members and some of the Saints who had arrived in California on the ship *Brooklyn* met in the Sierra Nevada foothills at a place they named Pleasant Valley. They began blazing a new trail *east* over the Sierras, leaving behind the newly

THE
LATTER-DAY SAINTS'
EMIGRANTS' GUIDE:

BEING A

TABLE OF DISTANCES,

SHOWING ALL THE

SPRINGS, CREEKS, RIVERS, HILLS, MOUNTAINS,

CAMPING PLACES, AND ALL OTHER NOTABLE PLACES,

FROM COUNCIL BLUFFS,

TO THE

VALLEY OF THE GREAT SALT LAKE.

ALSO, THE

LATITUDES, LONGITUDES AND ALTITUDES
OF THE PROMINENT POINTS ON THE ROUTE.

TOGETHER WITH REMARKS ON THE NATURE OF THE LAND,
TIMBER, GRASS, &c.

THE WHOLE ROUTE HAVING BEEN CAREFULLY MEASURED BY A ROADOME-
TER, AND THE DISTANCE FROM POINT TO POINT, IN
ENGLISH MILES, ACCURATELY SHOWN.

BY W. CLAYTON.

ST. LOUIS:

MO. REPUBLICAN STEAM POWER PRESS—CHAMBERS & KNAPP.
1848.

PROMINENT POINTS AND REMARKS.	Dist. miles.	From W Qrs. miles.	From C of G S L miles.
Sandy Bluffs, west foot. - - -	$\frac{1}{4}$	401$\frac{1}{4}$	629$\frac{3}{4}$
Dry creek. - - - -	$\frac{1}{4}$	401$\frac{1}{2}$	629$\frac{1}{2}$
Dry do. - - -	$\frac{3}{4}$	402$\frac{1}{4}$	628$\frac{3}{4}$
Dry creek, 30 feet wide. - - -	4	406$\frac{1}{4}$	624$\frac{3}{4}$
The road runs near the river, from here to Crab creek.			
Crab Creek, 20 feet wide, very shoal. -	3	409$\frac{1}{4}$	621$\frac{3}{4}$
Two miles further you will see some high bluffs on the right. By ascending one of the highest you will see Chimney Rock, to the west.			
Small lake, south of the road. -	1$\frac{1}{4}$	410$\frac{1}{2}$	620$\frac{1}{2}$
Good chance to camp, without turning from the road.			
Cobble Hills, east foot. - - -	5	415$\frac{1}{2}$	615$\frac{1}{2}$
You cross three dry creeks before you arrive here, and then you travel over another range of sandy bluffs—ascent pretty steep, but not very sandy.			
Cobble Hills, west foot. - - -	2$\frac{1}{4}$	417$\frac{3}{4}$	613$\frac{1}{4}$
After you descend on the low land, you will find it mostly sandy for ten miles, and in some places very heavy drawing.			
"Ancient Bluff Ruins," north side the road. Latitude 41° 33′ 3″.	1$\frac{1}{4}$	419	612
Resembling the ruins of ancient castles, fortifications, &c.; but visitors must be cautious, on account of the many rattle-snakes lurking round, and concealed in the clefts of the bluffs.			
R. and R., road joins the river. -	10$\frac{1}{2}$	429$\frac{1}{2}$	601$\frac{1}{2}$
Good place to camp. After this, the road runs near the river, until you arrive at the next low sandy ridges.			
Low sandy bluffs, east foot. -	7$\frac{1}{2}$	437	594
Low sandy bluffs, west foot. -	1	438	593
After this, the land for several miles, is soft in wet weather, but good traveling in dry weather.			
"Chimney Rock," (meridian) south side the river. - - -	14$\frac{1}{2}$	452$\frac{1}{2}$	578$\frac{1}{2}$
The higher land now begins to be sandy and barren. Many Prickly-pears and Wild Sage, which continue mostly through the remainder of the journey.			
Scott's Bluffs, (mer.) south side the river.	19$\frac{1}{2}$	472	559
The road here is near enough to the river to camp. Lat. of meridian. 41° 50′ 52″.; Long. 10? 20′.			
Spring Creek, 10 feet wide, 8 inches deep.	4	476	555
South of the road. You do not cross it, but travel half a mile alongside. Good water, and many trout in it.			
R. and R., road runs near the river. -	12$\frac{1}{2}$	488$\frac{1}{2}$	542$\frac{1}{2}$
Good chance to camp.			
Low sandy bluffs, north side the road. -	2$\frac{3}{4}$	491$\frac{1}{4}$	539$\frac{3}{4}$
You travel at the foot of these bluffs, but will find the road sandy and heavy on teams.			
Creek, about 200 yards south of road. -	2	493$\frac{1}{4}$	537$\frac{3}{4}$
By ascending one of the highest bluffs near, you have a view of "Laramie Peak" in the Black Hills.			
Timber, north side the river. - -	11$\frac{1}{2}$	504$\frac{3}{4}$	526$\frac{1}{4}$
Road here about a quarter of a mile from the river—after this, generally from one to two miles distant. The road, to Laramie, very sandy.			
"Raw Hide" creek, 1 rod wide. : -	5$\frac{1}{2}$	510	521
Plenty of water, June 1st, but dry, Sept. 15, 1847.			

discovered gold fields and making their way to fellow Church members already gathered in Salt Lake City.

Months before they started their eastward trek, six of these Battalion Boys—Henry Bigler, Azariah Smith, Alexander Stephens, James S. Brown, James Barger, and William Johnston—had participated in the discovery of gold at John Sutter's mill at Coloma. Like other Californians flush with gold fever, Battalion members quickly started collecting the precious metal from the American River, making a rich strike at a site known as Mormon Island. Despite their success, the Battalion Boys did not remain in the gold fields very long. For them, reuniting with families and friends in Salt Lake City and Council Bluffs took priority over quick riches.

To leave such an opportunity for easy wealth just as the gold rush was getting underway seems incredible. James S. Brown explained in his reminiscence:

"I have never seen that rich spot of earth since; nor do I regret it, for there always has been a higher object before me than gold. We [Mormon Battalion members] had covenanted to move together under certain conditions, and . . . we were honor bound to move the next day. We did move, leaving that rich prospect without ever sticking a stake in the gulch, but abandoning it to those who might follow. Some may think we were blind to our own interests; but after more than forty years we look back without regrets, although we did see fortunes in the land, and had many inducements to stay. . . . Still duty called, our honor was at stake, we had covenanted with each other, there was a principle involved; for with us it was God and His Kingdom first. We had friends and relatives in the wilderness, yea, in an untried, desert land, and who knew their condition? We did not. So it was duty before pleasure, before wealth."[4]

Among those at Pleasant Valley preparing to move east was a phenomenal woman, Melissa Coray. A newlywed,

Opposite: SALT LAKE CITY IN 1853, *Frederick Piercy.*
Below: MORMON BATTALION MEMBERS *at the fiftieth anniversary celebration of the discovery of gold, San Francisco, January, 1898. Left to right:* HENRY W. BIGLER, WILLIAM J. JOHNSTON, AZARIAH SMITH, *and* JAMES S. BROWN. *All these men were at Sutter's Mill when gold was discovered on January 24, 1848.*

she had refused to leave her Battalion husband, William, and completed the entire march from Winter Quarters to San Diego, then traveled north to Sacramento. She and William now prepared to traverse the Sierra Nevadas and the Great Basin to Salt Lake City.[5] Also among those gathering in Pleasant Valley were a few members of the ship *Brooklyn,* the Mormon immigrant ship that left New York for San Francisco in February 1846 with more than two hundred Saints under the leadership of Samuel Brannan. In total, forty-five men and Melissa began the eastward journey to their Zion in the Salt Lake Valley.

Because of the difficulty in taking wagons over Donner Pass and along the Truckee River so early in the season, they hoped to blaze an easier route through the mountains somewhere near the head of the American River. James S. Brown described both their reasoning and their confidence: "As we had become accustomed to pioneer life it was thought we could find a better route."[6]

Captain Samuel Thompson led the struggle over the Sierra Nevada, crossing the 9,500-foot Carson Pass. After a difficult descent along the West Fork of the Carson River, the company managed to reach the Carson Valley on August 4, 1848. Continuing along the Carson River for a

week, the pioneers headed north to the main California Trail. Behind them came other groups of former Mormon Battalion volunteers, also on their way to Salt Lake City.

As they followed the Humboldt River in what is today north central Nevada, the Thompson company encountered Samuel J. Hensley and a company of packers journeying west to California. The encounter proved important because Hensley's company had left from the Salt Lake Valley—the Thompson company's intended destination. A member of the Thompson company, Henry Bigler, recorded in his journal:

"We was met by Capt. S. Hinsley [and] a packing company of 10 men we got a way bill of our Road from here to salt lake and not [to] go by Ft Hall and save a bout 8 or 10 days travel. we learn from Mr. Hinsley that it is not more than a bout 380 miles to the lake [and] to take a serten cut off which we are sure to find with plenty of wood and water and grass [by] a route that he cum but waggons have never went there before a good waggon rout."[7]

Hensley, a Kentuckian by birth, followed the adventurous life of a trapper and mountain man. He came to California in the Chiles-Walker company of 1843 and briefly worked for John Sutter. After involvement in the Bear Flag Revolt for California's independence, he returned to the East for the court-martial trial of John C. Fremont.

Hoping to save time on his return trip to California, Hensley decided to travel to Salt Lake City on the Mormon Trail and then follow the Hastings cutoff south of the Great Salt Lake. Once he passed the lake and ventured out on the salt flats, heavy rains turned them into a hopeless mire, forcing his little band of ten to cut loose their packs and provisions from their animals and return with great difficulty to Salt Lake City, barely escaping with their lives.[8]

After reprovisioning, Hensley decided against another desert crossing. Instead he headed north, hoping to intersect the main California Trail. The strategy proved successful as he and his packers picked up the main trail near

Above: OLD SCOUT'S TALE, 1853, *William T. Ranney.*
Opposite: EMIGRATION TO THE WESTERN COUNTRY.

the City of Rocks in what is now southern Idaho. The trail he and his companions blazed proved significant because it became the preferred route for thousands of forty-niner gold-seekers who traveled the Mormon Trail into Salt Lake, rested, obtained provisions, and then joined the California Trail via Hensley's Salt Lake cutoff.

Many Mormons refused to believe the gold rush would end their vision of a Zion refuge. Melissa Coray,

THE GREAT SALT LAKE OF UTAH, *Thomas Moran.*

after suffering the rigors of the entire Mormon Battalion march and the journey across the Sierra Nevada to Salt Lake, had particular reason to view the valley as *the* refuge. In a letter to her sister in Illinois she wrote in October 1849, "I hope that in the many changes that have taken place that your mind and Elijah's is not changed in regard to Mormonism. I hope that you will make every exertion to come to the valley as soon as possible. If you was here you would not regret it for it will be the only place of safety

that can be found on earth, a resting place for the Saints."[9]

Although many Mormons, like Melissa, desired and prayed for a fulfillment of that vision, it vanished before an avalanche of argonauts seeking California gold.[10] The wall of isolation began to crumble almost as soon as the "City of the Saints" was platted. The resolution of the Mexican War not only brought vast areas of the West under U.S. control, but it also created the conditions for the establishment of new routes, such as Hensley's, to Salt Lake City.

This was the scene on the eve of the gold rush. A fleeing religious community, stung by years of bitter persecution and deadly hostility from neighbors, had established itself in a remote and relatively inaccessible valley on the edge of the Great Basin. While desiring some exchange with the broader American community, the Saints now assumed it would be on their terms. In their view, there would be no need or desire for anyone but Mormons to come to the valley of the Great Salt Lake. Knowing they were viewed with suspicion and distrust, they had little reason to expect anyone else to come to this isolated oasis. With the Pacific coast accessible by other routes, the Saints believed they would be left alone. However, the very success of their Rocky Mountain Zion, along with California gold, would soon shatter the illusion that they were insulated from a fast-changing world. Starting in 1849 and continuing for years, emigrants hoping to reach Zion traveled with emigrants hoping to reach their own promised land—California.

The emigration of 1849 simply astounded the nation. Newspaper accounts not only spoke of rich California mines but also noted the incredible numbers who planned to travel west. The Church newspaper, the *Millennial Star,* reported: "The amount of emigration over the Plains is immense, beyond all estimate. It is predicted there will be extreme distress and privation among the emigrating caravans. The average distance the teams travel per day is about 16 miles. There have been more than 20,000 mules, oxen and horses gone forth from Independence alone; from St. Joseph about 15,000; and the whole region at this moment seems like one tented field for miles and miles in all directions. There are more than 50,000 animals on the Plains at the very lowest estimate, and more than nine-tenths are traveling along the same track."[11]

The *Frontier Guardian* similarly communicated to its readers:

"They report the number of waggons that had passed Fort Childs [Kearney] up to the 15th inst., to be 7436 and like the ice at the breaking up of the Missouri, still coming. In addition to this number large numbers were seen to pass up on the north side of the Platte

Continued on page 89

STAMPEDE!

AMONG THE MANY DANGERS encountered on the trek west, stampedes were, according to an 1859 pioneer guide, "more to be dreaded upon the plains than almost any disaster that can happen."[13] Mules, horses, and oxen were all easily panicked. The animals stampeded for any one of a myriad reasons, including a deer or wolf passing by the camp at night, a rattlesnake, a pioneer shaking out clothes, dogs fighting, an electrical storm, or a buffalo stampede.

The potential consequences of the stampede included lost and crippled draft animals, broken wagons, killed or injured people, ruined provisions, and time lost in the laborious task of rounding up animals, fixing wagons, and caring for the wounded.

On July 30, 1850, Wilford Woodruff recorded these thoughts: "Our Encampment . . . was called to pass through one of those Horrid scenes to day which are so much dredded by all Emigrating Companies. . . . No person who has not Experienced or witnessed one of those dredful scenes cannot form any Correct idea of them . . . for to behold 30 or 40 ox teams [with] from 2 to five yoke of oxen in each team Attached to a family waggon of goods & women & Children All in an instant . . . each running their own way, roaring, bellowing rolling & tumbling over each other waggons upsetting smashing their wheels Exles & tongues spilling the goods women & Child in the street, for the next teams to trample under their feet as they roar & charge on their way with their yokes bows & chains flying in evry direction. . . . Little can be done at such times ownly for each one to dodge the best He can & save his own life if possible."[14]

John Powell recorded, "We noticed a great number of buffalo traveling towards the camp. As they came nearer, we shouted. They came faster, and to my great surprise they came to the train. Our oxen became frightened and as the buffalo passed the train, our teams took after them. . . . The buffalo took to the hills on the right of the road. The oxen kept up with them for about two miles. They then slacked their speed and finally stopped. . . . I came to a woman lying on the road, covered with blood. She had been run over by a wagon. I next came to a boy who had also been run over. I could not stay with them for I was troubled about the safety of my children who were walking by the train. . . . My wife was in the wagon. . . . I came to mine and saw an old lady standing at the head of the team, holding an umbrella before the eyes of the lead oxen. I thanked her. . . . I found my children. They ware safe. How they escaped being run over was a mystery. . . . I went back with several brethren and found the woman still lying in the same place. We bathed her face. . . . We then went to find the boy. We found him. . . . The wheels passed over his legs. We carried him to camp. This was the first stampede I had ever seen."[15]

BUFFALO STAMPEDE, *William H. Jackson.*

Continued from page 87

on the Mormon route. The upper route emigrants had no cholera or sickness among them."[12]

With such enormous numbers crossing the plains, Mormon companies would inevitably interact with non-Mormon gold seekers and share in the trials of emigrating west. In a letter to Orson Pratt, George A. Smith and William Appleby described the problems encountered during that season and gave a clear picture of the unusual nature of Mormon trains traveling west, often with European converts:"We left Winter Quarters on the 14th day of July, with about 130 wagons. . . . Capt. Owens (Judge Owens of Hancock county, Illinois) with a company of gold hunters, had a stampede a few weeks ago, about 70 miles from here, and lost upwards of 100 head. They were found near Fort Childs, by Captain Allen Taylor's company of Saints, and returned to them a few days after. The cattle travelled 130 miles in thirty-six hours. . . . We are composed of Yankees, English, Welsh, Norwegian, &c., yet we are one, although of different dialects and nations. . . . There are three companies of Saints a-head of us. . . . Capt. Samuel Gully went out last spring . . . on the 3rd day of August last we discovered his grave and another, Henry Vanderhoof, of the same company, but not a member of the church, neatly sodded over, and head boards with inscriptions upon them, about 180 miles from Winter Quarters, from which we learned that Brother Gully died of cholera, July 5th, 1849, and Vanderhoof on the 4th. We have also since learned with regret, from the gold diggers that returned after their lost cattle before referred to, that the same company at the Loup Fork, lost one man by drowning, another the Indians shot while out hunting. Four had died of cholera, and two more had been severely injured by cattle in a stampede. At Prairie Creek we saw the grave of an infant, son of Joseph Egbert, who died July 27th, 1849, aged seven months."[16]

California-bound gold seekers sometimes traveled with Mormon trains. Margaret Clawson described a stampede in her train involving a forty-niner:

"In that stampede there were two or three men hurt, one quite badly. He was a gold digger, going to California, who had overtaken us and was travelling with our company awhile. The California emigrants travelled much faster than the Mormon emigrants. In trying to stop the cattle this man was knocked down and trampled on, and his groans were piteous. I did not see him again until one day the next winter when he called on us. During all the time he was there he was down on his knees. He could stand up but could not sit down. I never heard from him again after he left for the gold mines."[17]

Along with the often-fatal accidents, cholera deaths would soon become a scourge that continued for several years. Although cholera was the most prevalent and dreaded disease, it was not the only deadly one on the trail. Somewhat vengefully, William Appleby recorded finding the grave of a Missouri emigrant:

Above: MARGARET GAY JUDD CLAWSON (1831–1912) journeyed to the Salt Lake Valley as a teenager in 1849.

"We here saw the grave of a gold digger, one E. Dodd (as the head board lying near the grave informed us) from Galatin county, Mo. Died July 19th, 1849 of typhoid fever. The wolves had completely disinterred him. The pantaloons, shirt, etc., in which he had been buried lay strewn around the grave. His under jaw bone lay in the bottom of the grave with the teeth all complete, and one of his ribs on the surface of the ground nearby were the only remains of him discoverable. It is believed he was the same Dodd that took an active part and was a prominent mobocrat in the murder of the Saints at Haun's Mill, Mo. If so, it is a righteous retribution, but he is not the only one whose graves and remains, believed to be mobocrats, that have been observed along the road over these boundless plains."[18]

While death and disease haunted many trains, others were barely touched. Still, the sight of hundreds of graves, often counted and recorded in journals, had a sobering effect on all travelers. The incidence of cholera diminished as the emigrants traveled farther west. However, new worries appeared as the trail system began to break down under the stress of unprecedented numbers of emigrants. Oxen and mule teams began to die from fatigue and poor feed, and the provisions of many ill-prepared emigrants began to run out. As they approached the Sublette Cutoff to head north to Fort Hall [in present-day southern Idaho], many increasingly desperate emigrants instead elected to continue west toward Fort Bridger and then Salt Lake, hoping to find fresh teams and more provisions.

Emigrants, if they had not encountered Mormons before, met them as soon as they reached the Upper Platte

and Green River ferries. Many diarists seemed surprised that the Mormons operating the ferries didn't match their poor image. William Johnston recorded, "Contrary to expectation, based upon the common reputation of these Latter-Day Saints, we found those in charge of the [Upper Platte] ferry, men of respectable appearance, well informed, polite, and in every way agreeable."[19] Traveling a few weeks behind Johnston, a Dr. Caldwell noted:

"Entered our names to cross when our turn comes. This is 5 miles below the old crossing, of Fremont & others. They have but one boat here, which is a good one, & very careful hands. The Mormons appear honest so far as dealing with them They conduct matters very well here, & have a smithery with 2 forges, but charge high. They are numerous at this place. Swim the cattle, & charge $3.00 per wagon for ferrying."[20]

According to Vincent Geiger, the enterprising Mormons "established a blacksmith shop here also at which they are making lots of money. So that with the ferry and shop they have as good a gold mine as any in California."[21]

Mormon emigrant Peter Hansen noted that gold fever had infected even the military whom he encountered at the Upper Platte ferry:

"Tuesday, July 3.

CROSSING THE SOUTH PLATTE, 1849.

"Cloudy, cool weather; we laid by to repair wagons, etc. Some of the troops going to Oregon and California were here trying to cross the river. More than half of them had deserted already and about half of the rest were fixing themselves up to leave likewise. It was a great joy that we met some of our brethren who were ferrying at this place."[22]

Emigrants found similar circumstances at the Green River crossing. Forty-niner Charles Darwin arrived at the Green in July and noted the increasing frustration of some of the less-patient emigrants wanting to cross: "Four dollars is the charge for wagons & fifty cents for packs & men. tho they do not hesitate to carry any one for nothing who is poor perfect gentlemen are they, in conversation conduct & entire bearing. they had been several of them in the mines & got gold & now lived at Salt Lake said that was the [nearer?] way. Many Ladies or such as look to be such were in a company crossing & some looked extremely fascinating. . . . Quite a comedy was enacted in my presence by a crowd who had a boat with them & thought to scare by vulgarity & show of crossing themselves the owner of the ferry with their terms he manfully & kindly resisted I was glad to see the rascals foiled I say rascals & their conduct justified the term."[23]

The sheer volume of traffic backed up wagon trains, causing bottlenecks at the ferries. Inevitably, competing ferries were soon established, and the Mormons no longer had a monopoly. Still, by any measure, this aspect of the gold rush proved profitable for the Saints. In addition to the Upper Platte and Green ferries, Mormons operated ferries at two locations on the Bear River and one on the Weber. An estimated 10,000 California-bound emigrants

Above: Fort Laramie, June 24, *James F. Wilkins, 1849.*
Opposite: Crossing the Plains—Journeying Zionward.

passed through Salt Lake City in 1849, and perhaps as many as 3,000 would-be argonauts wintered in the city. Trail traffic to Salt Lake was so heavy that one company "was held up for two hours in Emigration Canyon because of the accumulation of teams on the road."[24] Vincent A. Hoover arrived in Salt Lake City in mid-August and noted the difficult conditions:

"There is reported a great deal of suffering on Subletts Cut Off. The mormons have Sent relief trains. . . . We have concluded to take Southern route [to California]

there is not grass on the northern. We will have to delay here six weeks [so] we would have time to go through but so many have gone through [on the northern route] that we are afraid to try it. We also Learn that the mormons have sent on oxen to the emigrants that are suffering on the sublets cut off."[25]

Latter-day Saints and gold-seeking emigrants recorded their reactions to one another. While in Salt Lake City in July 1849, Ben Carpenter wrote to his father in Indiana:

"I arrived here yesterday night after a long and tedious journey of 1250 mil[es] taking two months and a half to accomplish. . . . We did not at first expect to come this way, but afterward learned it to be the best and nearest route. West from the city we are to take . . . a new route via the *North end* of the Salt Lake. this route has only been traviled by Mormons. they say it is a good road & plenty of grass & water. only a small portion of the emigration come this way, by far the greatest [number] taking *Sublettes cut off* thence to Fort Hall & down to the old track to California. I have great fear for those behind us. I cannot see how they are to subsist their stock the grass was gone when we came along, and we are by no means among the last. The proprietor of the Ferry at Greene River told me that 300 waggons had camped the lower Ferry & upwards of 1600 at the Upper Ferry. . . . I have seen men with pack mules that left the 'States' as late as the 29th of May they estimate the [number] of waggons behind at between 4 & 5 thousand."[26]

Writing three days earlier, also to relatives in Indiana, Salt Lake City resident William Scearce gave his less-than-generous opinion of the forty-niners: "Now for the gold digers it is about five weeks Since the first train arived in the vally Since which time they have been ariving nearly every day and not more than one out of twenty Comes this way the others going by the way of fort hall poor fellows they are learning very fast & the most of them have learnt so much that if they were at home again they would Stay there. . . . they are right glad to get once more into Civilization where they can get good butter & cheese & vegitables & exchange their wagons & some of their bacon & flour & coffee & sugar & clothing & impliments for gold diging, for horses & mules & pack saddles & lassoes. thus equipt they . . . go on to the great theater where will be [enacted?] many new senes of iniquity: on the east of this [valley] they have thrown away & Destroyed thousands of dollars worth of property in their [race to outdistance] others in their travel to the gold digings."[27]

If some Mormons disliked the emigrants and their gold-digging objectives, they could do little about it; by the same token some emigrants found life among the Saints not to their liking. Forty-niner Arthur Shearer summed up his opinion of the Mormons: "They call us Gentiles and regard themselves as [entitled] to superior privileges. They are more troublesome beggars than the savages and to take the united voice of the emigrants for it they are worse thieves. They [the emigrants] believe that."[28]

Unlike Shearer, George Withers found life in Salt Lake City enjoyable: "I have been very hospitably treated by the Mormons since I have been here. I believe them to be a generous and hospitable people and all the emigrants speak well of them."[29] When it came to the Mormons, it was apparent that each emigrant saw what he or she wanted to see.

The number who passed through Salt Lake City in 1850, estimated at fifteen thousand, was more than the number of permanent residents in the city. The 1850

emigration replicated on an even greater scale what had occurred in 1849. Conditions on the trail turned catastrophic. The sheer volume of wagon traffic along the trail stripped all available feed for draft animals. Reports of increasing difficulties on the main trail beyond South Pass, cholera and other illnesses, want and necessity, general weariness with trail travel, and perceptions of the virtues of the Salt Lake Cutoff all contributed to diverting travelers to an increasingly overburdened Salt Lake City.

With far greater numbers traveling west in 1850, there was a correspondingly higher death toll from cholera, which again stalked the trail. Samuel Gifford, traveling in the second Mormon train of the season, described the company's dubious good fortune of having only "just five and no more" die:

"The Cholera also commenced its work in camp and soon we burried a gentile that died of the Cholera and then Peter Shirts' wife died. Then Captain Thomas Johnson called the camp together and said 'If you will do as I tell you with regard to the water that you use for drinking I will promise you that there shall not more than five die in this camp with the Cholera.['] All believed what he said and did accordingly and the strange promise was literally fulfilled, for just five and no more died. While the gold seekers ahead of us and the Saints behind us were dying at a fearful rate. I will now tell about the water. The Platte water being muddy, there had been wells dug all along the Platte bottom to get clear water. The wells were about six feet deep with steps dug to get to the water. The

council was this, 'To not go near those wells for water but get their water out of the river and drink none without boiling and to fill their churns, teakettles, and everything that they had that would hold water with boiled water to use while traveling.['] There was in the camp a kind of a fearful looking for the Small pox, as quite a number had been exposed, but no one had it. The Lord had respects to the words of his servant and preserved the camp from farther sickness and death."[30]

Thomas Steed, traveling in the first Mormon company of the season, described the lack of feed for stock as well as the incidence of cholera among the wagon trains of gold seekers:

"The gold fever prompted many to go to California that summer, by way of the north side of the Platte, so that the feed for animals was all used up. For that reason President [Orson] Hyde advised us to go along the south side. Some of the gold seekers did take the same route. The cholera broke out among them; they were all around us—before us and behind us, although we tried to keep away from them, and many of them died; but our company escaped."[31]

Not all Mormon companies were so lucky. George Bryant Gardner, traveling with the Wilford Woodruff company, the eighth Mormon company of the season, noted the ravages of cholera on his fellow travelers:

"We traveled in Brother Wilford Woodruff's company. . . . We reached the road on the south side of Platt River. After being out a few days cholera made its appearance in our train. There had been a train of gold hunters who passed us on their way to California, which had the cholera. We counted from 20 to 100 graves in a days travel. Many graves had been robbed by wolves and the skeletons of the poor victims were scattered on the ground. We lost 16 adults and 1 child who died of cholera before we reached Fort Kearney."[32]

Crossing the plains as a young boy, Joseph Fish recalled, "My father walked nearly every step of the way he counted the graves as we passed along getting up to a little over a thousand when he gave it up being taxed with a give out team and other things which occupied his attention. . . . To cheer us on the way the popular song 'Come come ye saints no toil nor labor fear but with joy wend your way' was sung quite often with other songs of a cheering character."[33]

Ten Mormon companies, numbering about five thousand, traveled the trail to Salt Lake in 1850. In contrast, an estimated fifty thousand people headed west that year, most for California. Despite increasing difficulties, Joseph Fish recalled the beginning of his journey with a certain measure of romantic innocence:

"As the company stretched out across the broad prairies it presented a picturesque appearance. Bare-footed children, here and there, wending their way along the line of march. Women, some with sunbonnets, some with hats and others with various kinds of protection for the head, traveling along through the hot dust and over the parched plains. Men with their long whips walking beside the lolling oxen that were dragging their heavy loads towards the setting sun. A variety of characters were behind bringing up the rear with the loose stock which was varied as their drivers. All were hastening west as fast as they could over these boundless prairies."[34]

This impression faded and was replaced by other images, such as his father's grave counting. By the time many emigrant trains reached the Sweetwater River, their draft animals began to fail. Emigrants began discarding everything that was not needed to lighten the load on their animals and to increase speed. Samuel Gifford

PLATTE RIVER NEAR FORT KEARNEY, William H. Jackson.

wrote a graphic account of the rapidly expanding trail junkyard:

"The horror that reigned in camps ahead of us cannot be described. Sometimes (places) for miles could be seen, feather beds, blankets, quilts, and clothing of every kind strewed over the plains, also wagon tires and irons of every description, gun barrels, stoves, etc. etc. The bottom of the Sweetwater was also lined with wagon tires, chains and other irons. And fresh graves could be seen in every direction. We met some missionaries going east who said they met companies of the gold emigration that were driving twelve abreast, hurrying to get away from the Cholera."[35]

Joseph Fish recalled a similar scene:

"On August 4th we arrived at the Devil's Gate. At this place we found quite a number of wagons. Several had been burnt. The emigrants going to the mines of California had found it impossible to take all their wagons and loading through, so some left their wagons and others burnt them rather than have them fall into the hands of the Mormons. They were eager to get through to the mines on the coast, and wagons, give out animals and innumerable articles of all kinds were left by the wayside. I even noticed an old broken fiddle. The road along here was lined with these articles as they had been thrown aside to lighten the loads of those who were hastening to the Elderado of the west."[36]

The trail trash that Fish saw became a windfall for the Mormons in Salt Lake City. Church leaders organized scavenging hunts to recover usable goods discarded by passing emigrant trains. John D. Lee reported finding

DEVIL'S GATE, 1858.

"Harness, Tools of Every discription, Provisions, clothings, stoves, cooking vessels, Pouder, Lead, & all most everything, etc. that could be mentioned."[37] While collecting the discarded windfall, Lee became a beacon of hope to passing non-Mormon emigrant trains:

"Very frequent[ly] some 20 or 30 persons would suround the waggon and plead for a memonts [moment's] instructions, some of them with consternation depicted on their countenances, their teams worn out, wumen & children on foot & som packing their provision[s], trying to reach Some point of Refuse [refuge]. The general cry was, are you from the Mormon city or vally? Yes. What is the distance? Is there any feed by the way? What will be the cha[r]ge to get fresh animals, Provisions, vegitables, Butter, cheese, &c. could we winter in the vally? Do pray tell us all you can that will benefit us, for we are in great distress. Stop & write us a way bill. We will pay you all you ask. Apples, Peaches (Dried), coffee, sugar, Tea, Rice, Flour, Bacon, &c., was often brought & presented. . . . Truly one of the ancient[s] said that the love of money was the Root of all Evil. It was the love of it that has caused thousands to leave their pleasant homes & comfortable Firesides & thus plunge themselves into unnessary suffering & distress."[38]

Some Latter-day Saints claimed that much of the suffering on the trail fell on travelers from Missouri and Illinois, whom they felt were responsible for much of their previous suffering. William Butler noted, "This year there was great destruction of life and property among the people, mostly of Illinois and Missouri, who were traveling on the Plains to the gold mines of California."[39]

Latter-day Saints often became nervous about the new emigrants. Nelson Whipple noted that his captain did not relax until they were beyond South Pass and most of the emigrants had taken the Sublette Cutoff to Fort Hall: "After we past the South Pass as it is cald the captin told his Company that if

Above: NELSON WHIPPLE (1818–1887), Mormon emigrant.
Left: GEORGE A. SMITH (1817–1875), an apostle and a good friend of Brigham Young. Photographer: Charles R. Savage.

they felt like dancing to dance and injoy them Selves as he felt as though we was deliverd from under the hands of our Enimies who would not have the power to abuse us as they had before done."[40]

Just as some Mormons feared the non-Mormon emigrants, the reverse was also true. Missourians felt a particular need to stay clear of Salt Lake and stick to the Fort Hall route. In a reminiscent account of his 1850 overland journey, Isaac Harvey wrote, "I went north of Salt Lake City as the Mormons were down on Missourians generally and many Missouri trains got into trouble. If their stock got into gardens or any fields they were fined heavily. It was charged that Mormons would turn the cattle in on purpose to make trouble. I knew many emigrants that were ruined and had to work their way to Oregon or California."[41]

Apostle George A. Smith painted a different picture of Mormon reaction to former enemies:

"The very men who were the murderers of our fathers, and our brothers, the burners of our houses, have come here among this people since that time, where they have received protection; they have been fed when they were hungry. The very man who burned the house of Elder Moses Clawson, at Lima, came to him and said, 'Mr. Clawson, I want to get some provisions from you.' Now these very persecutors knew that our religion was true, and that we were men of sterling integrity, or else they never would have thrown themselves in our way, and called upon us for aid afterwards; and I am proud to say, that kind aid and assistance on their journey to the gold mines, have been extended to hundreds of these robbers, and thus the coals of fire have been heaped upon their heads; but their skulls were so thick, it never burned many of them a bit."[42]

George A. Smith verbalized a growing realization that such increased contact inevitably brought back old tensions and suspicions. Still, the Mormon community recognized the economic good fortune that the gold discovery brought to the Salt Lake Valley. The emigration provided them with a ready market, cheap manufactured goods, and real profits. John D. Lee recorded the effect of the emigration on the Salt Lake economy:

"Waggons that was rating from 50 to 125 dols. before the Emigration commenced roling in, were sold & traded during the summer & fall of 1849 from 15 to 25 dollars; Harness from 2 to 15 dollars (Per) set. Oxen, Cows, Horse, Mules, &c were sold & exchanged upon the most reasonable terms. Fresh Horses & mules were soon raised to $200 each, so great was the demand for them. Most of the Emigrants abandoned their waggons when they reached the Valley such as had not befor & proceeded with Pack animals. Coffee & Sugar which had been selling at [$]1.00 Per Pint was frequently sold at from 10 to 15 cts.; Bacon the Same; first rate Sacked Hams at 12 1/2 cts. Lb. & Dry goodes & clothing below the State Prices."[43]

George Mayer, a relatively poor Mormon living in Salt Lake City, summarized the personal effect of the emigration:

"[In 1850] my clothe[s] ware nerly all wore out and I dident no ware the others wolde Come from, But, the Golde Minse [mines] being open in Caleforny brote a Large Emegration throo our Towne, and the[y] Solde there wagons and ther things that they Colde [could] not pack to our pepel very Cheepe and gave many things away—

The[y] fild our town with wagons and hors harnes and Clothing of all kinds, of mens Clothing and Store goods of Every kinde. I went to worke and made 100 and 10 pack Sadels and Solde them for $2.00 Dollers - $5.00 Dollers apese and I was abel to By me a fine horse teme and a nother yoke of oxen."[44]

Beyond individual benefit, Joseph Holbrook saw the gold rush as providential to all of Mormon society:

"And thus in a few years in this desolated part of the mountains we were beginning to enjoy to some degree that which might have taken years had not the Lord provided for the poor saints by His providence in opening up the gold mines in California and inspiring the Gentiles with a lust for gold."[45]

Above: GEORGE MAYER (1805–1896), 1848 Mormon pioneer and farmer.
Right: HEBER C. KIMBALL (1810–1868), c. 1855. Apostle, pioneer, and counselor to Brigham Young.

BUFFALO CROSSING THE MISSOURI RIVER, *William De La Montague Cary. The clash between cultures and the coming change is symbolically represented as the Indian awaits the buffaloes' arrival and the white man steams upriver.*

Likewise, George Washington Hill saw a fulfillment of prophecy in the gold discovery: "We now began to realize the fullfillment of a prophesy of Heber C. Kimbals made the fall before the second emmigration. the people were in a very Destitute condition. heber came out on the stand and in the name of Israels god [prophesied] that in less than twelve months every thing we needed in the provision, grocery and dry goods line should be bought in the streets of Salt lake cheaper than it would cost in St Louis. he said himself afterwards he was scared for he said it before he knew what he was saying but it was now being fulfilled for the emmigrants came flocking in by thousands loaded down. why they had loaded so heavey they did not know but now they were in a hurry to get to the gold mines before the gold was all got and they would pay fabulous prices for . . . ponyes and would sell anything they [could for] just what they could get. in some instances they would give a new wagon and three or four yoke of cattle and out-fit for a pony that one month before could have been bought for twenty five dollars. there were, just as heber saw it would be, ready made clothing calicos, domestics, flour, bacon, powder, lead and almost every thing that we wanted sold at less than st Louis prices. and then they Brought the money along for us to buy their goods with and gave it to us for a few ponyes, a little garden sauce, butter and milk and so on so that by the time the emmigration was over the majority of the people were quite comfortable and Hebers prophecy had been fulfilled to the fullest extent."[46]

Yet, despite the economic benefits, there were many

negative aspects to the wave of non-Mormons that descended on Salt Lake City. The stock of passing emigrant trains devoured local forage to such an extent that the Saints had to establish New England–style commons and assign herdsmen as guards to ensure that there would be enough feed for their own animals.[47] While loss of forage was detrimental to established families, spiraling prices were crushing to newly arrived Mormon emigrants. By June 1850, still early in the emigration season, flour in Salt Lake City sold for $50.00 per hundred pounds, and corn meal $25.00 per hundred pounds.[48]

Mormon difficulties with Native Americans also increased proportionately with the increased emigrant traffic on the Salt Lake Cutoff and the Oregon-California Trail. Great Basin tribes suffered as their traditional food supplies disappeared, leaving them little choice but to engage in activities that were unacceptable to whites, such as poaching draft animals from emigrant trains. One newspaper correspondent wrote in June 1855 that "the overland emigration to California has scared away the game, so that [Native Americans] have to live on fish and reptiles." Mormons made attempts to feed some Indians, but in the late 1850s and early 1860s relations between the settlers and the natives continued to deteriorate.

Another drawback to the emigration came in the form of an unexpected health-service burden. So many emigrants left their sick and dying with the Mormons as they hurried toward the California mines that the Church leadership instituted a quarantine system for the sick and the stock of emigrant trains entering the Salt Lake Valley: "Hitherto, California emigrants have been accus-

NOTICE

TO THE

EMIGRANTS!!!

I take this method of notifying all persons, en route for California that the Indians on Mary's river, heretofore, have been very hostile, and committed many depredations upon the Emigrants, by stealing cattle, horses, &c., and killing many of the travelers, and will most probably prove troublesome this season, unless due

Caution and Vigilance

Is used, in passing through their country.

Maj. Holeman, the Indian Agent for this Territory, has gone in that direction, and will, it is hoped, effect peaceful relations with them. It is, however, best to be on the alert, and not give them any advantage.

It would be wisdom to travel in companies large enough, so that a vigilant guard can be kept up without being so burdensome upon the men, as to wear them out, and render them unfit for service; to have your arms and ammunition in order, and ready for instant use; to select your camping places as remote as possible from brush or any other covert place.

Either tie up your stock within your guard encampment at night, or have a guard constantly out with them. It is also best for each organized company to keep together, as those straggling from camp may be molested. It is confidently believed if a little caution, and strict vigilance is used, all may go safely; and being notified, will be prepared accordingly. But little danger is apprehended until after passing Goose creek mountains, as the Shoshone or Snake Indians have heretofore been very friendly, so much so, that one man could travel in their country in peace and safety. I therefore request all travelers, in order to sustain peaceful relations with them, to treat them kindly.

Given under my hand at Great Salt Lake City, Utah Territory, the twelfth day of June, 1852.

BRIGHAM YOUNG, Governor,

And ex-officio Superintendent of Indian Affairs, Utah Territory

pality, quarantine has been introduced, and no animals are permitted to roam within the corporation . . . ; and when the surrounding lands are fenced, the accommodations in our vicinity, for those who travel by multitudes will be small, indeed; and we believe that it will be more convenient for the great mass of travellers to the mines to go by Fort Hall, or some other route north of this, saving to themselves the expense and hindrance of quarantine, and other inconveniences arising from a temporary location near a populous city, where cattle are not permitted to run at large."[49]

This proved to be some annoyance for John Clark, who was traveling to California in 1852. On arrival in the valley he wrote:

"Eight o'clock and we are on the borders of the great valley. Quarantine ground lies at the gate of this can[y]on and here is a hospital, or what pretends to be one, established by Governor Young, where all, both great and small, Jew or Gentile, are obliged to report. Those who are well are privileged to continue their journey, but what they do with the sick or disabled I am unable to say. I saw none, and as the hospital building is barely large enough to hold the doctor, a barrel of whiskey and a few decanters, I can safely say there were no sick or

tomed to leave their sick in our hands, at a very heavy expense and depart without notice; to turn their teams loose in our streets, and near our city, which has caused so much destruction of crops and grass, so that if we want a load of hay, we have to go from ten to twenty miles to procure it, and drive our cattle a still greater distance to herd the winter; but since the organization of a munici-

disabled emigrants within its walls. The doctor was busily employed in dealing out whiskey and appeared to have a good run of custom in that way, but how many sick emigrants he attended to I did not stop to inquire."[50]

Much to Brigham Young's consternation, the emigrants also created a restlessness among some of the Mormons, who began considering the benefits of California gold mining. In his plain-speaking manner he thundered, "If you Elders of Israel want to go to the gold mines, go and be damned."[51]

Ultimately, Church leaders faced a new reality of their fledgling Zion. Beginning with the gold rush of 1849, the Mormon hope of *fleeing* to an isolated Zion vanished forever. The existence of the Mormon Trail, so essential in establishing their refuge, was instrumental in ending their isolation as well. Future Mormon emigrants would now *gather* to Zion, and as they came to the Salt Lake Valley, they would always be sharing the Mormon Trail with others whose hopes and dreams lay even farther to the west. ✳

LIFE ON THE TRAIL

Sights, Sounds, and Smells

〜〜〜

EMIGRANTS TRAVELING to the Salt Lake Valley had novel experiences that were often hard for them to describe. The open vistas and endless prairie, strange geological features, countless buffalo, prairie-dog towns, Native Americans, and even other emigrants from every walk of life were just some of the unusual sights the Zion-bound emigrants encountered. Surviving journals and diaries reveal their efforts at describing these new and amazing scenes.

The continuous sight of the Platte River and its potential for farming were not lost on emigrants like Levi Jackman. He was accustomed to seeing the hardwood forests of the East, and the lack of timber on the plains must have seemed remarkable to him. He wrote, "We hav came up the Platte & Loupe fork about 130 miles throug as fine a Countrey as I ever saw. almost entirely level, the finest Countrey for farming that can be with the exception of timber. cotton wood skirting the river is all the timber to be found and verrey scarse at that."[52]

Views of the mountains impressed many emigrants, including Abner Blackburn. As he approached the Salt Lake Valley, he and two of his Battalion companions "undertook to climb a high mountain in sight of the camp to take a view of the surrounding country." He wrote,

"Passed the timber line far enough [and] landed on the sumit [of] the highest peak in sight. [It was] the grandest view that ever mortal beheld. The air was clear and perfect for a good view—the Great Salt Lake glittering under the suns rays, range after range of mountains in every direction, the great desert to the west and Utah Lake to the south east and the mountains beyond. A more sublime view was seldom seen from a mountain top."[53]

Traveling in the Benjamin Gardner Company, Jonathan Ellis Layne also wrote of his encounter with the mountains: "It was a new thing for us to climb the mountains, the different kinds of timber, pine and spruce, the magnificent mountain scenery and views to be had were so entirely new to me and I greatly enjoyed it. In after years in Utah I grew to love it with all my heart."[54] Flowers, not just mountains, caught the eye of Lucy Meserve Smith. After surviving the difficult winter at Winter Quarters in 1846, she remained in the Midwest for three years, finally emigrating in 1849. While near Scotts Bluff, she felt a tinge of homesickness, remarking, "We passed some very beautiful flower gardens, resembling fields of red clover. It makes me think of home."[55]

In addition to the new and different topography, animals both large and small captured the attention of the emigrants. As the train passed Grand Island, Richard Ballantyne wrote of the prairie-dog towns he saw: "During the last two day we passed a number of very large Prarie Dog Towns. They seem to locate their Towns on gentle elevations of land and live on grass. They are about the size of Cats or small puppies and are of a brownish color."[56] Of course, nothing could compare to the sight of a moving buffalo herd. Like so many emigrants, John Pulsipher described them with a sense of awe: "Thousands of them sometimes would run towards the River, plunge down the bank into the water, tumble over each other and pile up, but all would come out right on the other side of the River and continue the race. Sometimes we would see the Plain black with them for ten miles in width and I don't know how far beyond our sight they extended, all in motion, on the gallop and would pass by us for hours at that speed and then we could see neither end of the herd."[57]

Dead animals, usually emigrant stock left to rot, were not something most wanted to see. More than the sight, Emigrants undoubtedly wished they could forget the smell. Sometimes the unwelcome odor brought an additional unwelcome sight: wolves. At Independence Rock, Rachel Simmons recalled, "The companies ahead of us lost a great many animals at this place. The stench was awful, and the wolves were as thick as sheep. It seemed as though they had gathered for miles around. . . . They were so bold they would come right into camp and some of them would put their feet on the wagon tongues and sniff in at the end of the wagon."[58] A disagreeable smell sometimes came from tragedy. When Jacob Weatherby was killed, Patty Sessions noted that his body "was calculated to be caried back to Winter Quarters to bury him but he mortified and smelt so bad they buried him in a buffalo robe near the liberty pole."[59]

Some sounds were new to the emigrants, including the howling of wolves. Thomas Bullock wrote, "The wolves kicked up a regular rumpus during the night; as quick as they commenced howling the dogs barked, the cattle lowed, and men shouted to call their loose cattle together."[60] Indian cries and gunfire were sounds no one wanted to encounter, but a few times they were heard. One morning, shortly after leaving Winter Quarters and before he had even reached the Elkhorn River, Norton Jacob "heard some Indians whooping and a gun fired." He wrote, "Soon four of them came to us and were very saucy because we would not give them our provisions. One of them offered to shoot one of our cows, but they finally went away by our giving them two ears of corn apiece."[61]

Young Parley P. Pratt, Jr., summarized both the familiar and new in what he saw on the trail, recalling, "New scenes burst upon our view, and now and again we would meet the hunter and the trapper or a band of Indians decked with beads, ornaments and feathers. The novelty and bustle of camp life, the neighing of the horses, the lowing of the cows with their young calves, the deer, antelope, and buffalo and flocks of wild geese, the rocks, rills and caves, the lone tree by the wayside, the cold spring, the oasis in the desert, the Indian wickiup and grave, the wild flowers and laughing children, the prairie fires and moonlight nights, the howling wolves and screeching night owls, the inspired Sabbath address and song of Zion, all filled my young heart with delight and inspiration."[62]

Still, despite the new sounds, sights, and smells the emigrants encountered, perhaps the ones they cherished the most were those that were most familiar. At a campsite just beyond Fort Kearney, Hezekiah Mitchell wrote, "All is life and activity when cooking, watching, singing, talking, laughing and little boys and girls are running, jumping, skipping about camp, a great work and a wonder." The impressions of the trip would never leave the emigrants, but neither would the associations and family relationships that were forged and strengthened in the greatest adventure of their lives—traveling the Mormon Trail.

GATHERING TO ZION

THE CALIFORNIA GOLD RUSH brought unprecedented income to the Church, income that Brigham Young quickly used in creative efforts to encourage emigration. Emigrants were important to the plans of Church leaders, who were essentially creating a new society in the Great Basin. They needed the thousands of American Saints comfortably settled near the banks of the Missouri and the rapidly increasing number of converts in Europe to gather to Utah and help build this new religious kingdom. Most gold seekers passing through the fledgling Mormon community intended to spend as little time as possible in California acquiring gold before returning to the "States." Mormon emigrants knew that emigrating to Salt Lake City often meant cutting all ties to their nativity, to friends and family, and to their past. For most, their commitment was total, based on religious faith and tied to a hope for a better life, economic as well as spiritual.

Throughout the 1850s Brigham Young and other leaders experimented with ways to perfect an immigration sys-

tem that would meet the needs of the Church. Still, all their efforts would have been futile were it not for the willingness of faithful Mormon emigrants to sacrifice *everything* to build up what they considered to be the kingdom of God on earth. After the handcart disasters of 1856, Mormon emigration became increasingly more systematic. By the 1860s it had become a well-oiled machine, and the organizational wonder of the Church "down-and-back" train system would bring tens of thousands to the Valley of the Great Salt Lake in relative comfort and safety.

However, in 1849, with Church coffers swelling from the gold-rush economic windfall, it began to appear that transporting thousands of emigrants would be reduced to a simple issue of financing their passage. Proposed by Brigham Young in September 1849 and submitted and approved in the Church's general conference of 1849, the Perpetual Emigrating Fund, or P.E.F., became an integral

Opposite: EMIGRANTS CROSSING THE PLAINS, *H. B. Hall.*

Brigham Young, c. 1857.

part of the Church's plan to encourage emigration. The company received formal approval to incorporate by the legislative assembly of the newly established State of Deseret in September 1850.

Brigham Young was elected president of the P.E.F., a position he held for the rest of his life. The stated purpose of the company was "to promote, facilitate, and accomplish the Emigration of the Poor." Monies loaned were considered just that, loans—not gifts. The fund's promoters claimed, "This will make the honest in heart rejoice, for they love to labor . . . and not live on the charity of their friends: while the lazy idlers, if any such there be, will find fault . . . and in the end pay nothing. The Perpetual Fund will help no such idlers; we have no use for them in the valley; they had better stay where they are."[1]

In matters of emigration, Brigham Young and his counselors, comprising the First Presidency of the Church, focused first on the thousands of American Saints still nestled on the banks of the Missouri. Following the October 1849 conference, the presiding bishop of the Church, Edward Hunter, carried a letter from the First Presidency to Apostle Orson Hyde in Iowa outlining the purpose of the Perpetual Emigrating Fund:

"The Lord has been devising, or rather making manifest ways and means to facilitate the gathering of His Saints in these last days, and we lose no time in cheering your heart with the intelligence, and offering such suggestions as may be wisdom for you to follow, in helping to roll on the glorious work of gathering Israel. . . . We write to you . . . at this time, concerning the gathering, and the mission of our general agent, for the PERPETUAL

EMIGRATING FUND. . . . The few thousands we send out by our agent, at this time is like a grain of mustard seed in the earth; we send it forth into the world, and among the Saints, a good soil; and we expect it will grow and flourish, and spread abroad in a few weeks so that it will cover England, cast its shadow in Europe, and in the process of time compass the whole earth: that is to say, these funds are designed to increase until Israel is gathered from all nations, and the poor can sit under their own vine and inhabit their own house, and worship God in Zion."[2]

In the fall of 1851, the First Presidency issued another circular intended to shake the Saints loose from the Midwest. The Church had been established in the Salt Lake Valley for more than five years, and still many members would not emigrate. Church leaders employed some blunt language in their efforts to convince the Saints on the Missouri to head for the Valley: "O ye Saints in the United States, will you listen to the voice of the good Shepherd? Will you gather? Will you be obedient to the heavenly commandments? Many of you have been looking for, and expecting too much; you have been expecting the time would come, when you could journey across the mountains in your fine carriages, your good wagons, and have all the comforts of life that heart could wish; but your expectations are vain, and if you wait for those things you will never come, . . . and your faith and hope will depart from you. How long shall it be said in truth 'the children of this world are wiser in their generation than the children of light.' Some of the children of the world, have crossed the mountains and plains, from Missouri to California, with a pack on their back to worship their

COUNCIL BLUFFS FERRY, IOWA, *Frederick Piercy.*

god—Gold. Some have performed the same journey with a wheel-barrow, some have accomplished the same with a pack on a cow. Some of the Saints, now in our midst, came hither with wagons or carts made of wood, without a particle of iron, hooping their wheels with hickory, or raw hide, or ropes, and had as good and safe a journey as any in the camps, with their well wrought iron wagons; and can you not do the same? Yes, if you have the same desire, the same faith. Families might start from Missouri river, with cows, hand-carts, wheel-barrows, with little flour, and no unnecessaries, and come to this place quicker, and with less fatigue, than by following the heavy trains, with their cumbrous herds, which they are often obliged to drive miles to feed. Do you not like this method of travelling? Do you think salvation costs too much? If so, it is not worth having. Sisters, fifty and sixty years old, have drove ox teams to this valley, and are alive and well yet; true they could have come much easier by walking alone, than by driving a team, but by driving the oxen, they helped others here; and cannot you come the easier way? There is grain and provision enough in the Valleys for you to come to; and you need not bring more than enough to sustain you one hundred days, to ensure you a supply for the future."[3]

The First Presidency also dispatched Apostles Ezra T. Benson and Jedediah M. Grant to assist in the emigration, adding, "Come to this place with them next season; *and fail not.* . . . There is no more time for Saints to hesitate what course they will pursue. We have been calling to the Saints in Pottawatamie ever since we left them to come away; but there has continually been an opposing spirit, whispering, as it were—Stay another year, and get a better fit-out, until many who had means to come conveniently have nothing left to come with. . . . We say again, come home! And if you can get one good wagon and team to five families, and five teams to one hundred souls; or no teams at all, more than cows and calves to your handcarts, you can come here with greater comfort and safety than the Pioneers came here who had nothing to come to; while you will have every thing; and here is the place for all the Saints to get their fit-out for Zion, even from all nations, therefore we say again, *Arise and Come home.*"[4]

Far left: EZRA T. BENSON (1811–1969), c. 1853. Mormon apostle sent to the Midwest to encourage Saints to emigrate to Utah. Photographer: Marsena Cannon. Left: JEDEDIAH M. GRANT (1816–1856), first mayor of Salt Lake City, sent with Ezra T. Benson to aid in emigration effort. Right: MISSIONARIES IN GREAT BRITAIN, 1855. The occasion of this photograph was a meeting to discuss the possibilities of using handcarts to move poor Mormon emigrants from the Missouri River to Utah. Top row, left to right: Edmund Ellsworth, Joseph A. Young, William H. Kimball, George D. Grant, James Ferguson, James A. Little, Philemon Merrill. Middle row: Edmund Bunker, Chauncey Webb, Franklin D. Richards, Daniel Spencer, Dan Jones, Edward Martin. Bottom row: James Bond, Spicer Crandall, W. Dunbar, James Ross, Daniel McArthur.

Their efforts paid off handsomely. The spring of 1852 saw the largest exodus of Latter-day Saints on the Mormon Trail in any of its twenty-two year existence. The emigration of these Saints was deemed so important that Church leaders took an unprecedented step, one that probably never has been and never will be repeated—the virtual suspension of calling new missionaries:

"Viewing the gathering of Israel, which produces our increased population in the valleys of the mountains, an important part of the gospel of Jesus Christ, and one of the most important at the present time, we shall send few, or no Elders abroad to preach the gospel this fall; but instruct them to raise grain and build houses, and prepare for the Saints, that they may come in flocks, like doves to their windows; and we say, arise! to your wagons and your tents, O scattered Israel! ye Saints of the Most High! rich and poor, and gather to the State of Deseret, bringing your plows and drills, your reapers and gleaners, your threshers and cleaners of the most approved patterns, so that one man can do the labor of twenty in the wheat field, and we will soon send the Elders abroad by hundreds and thousands to a harvest of souls among the nations, and the inhabitants of the earth shall speedily hear of the salvation prepared by Israel's God for His people."[5]

By the fall of 1852, with most of the "American" Saints now residing in the valley or in colonies the Church began establishing throughout the west, attention turned to the European Saints. That year also saw the number of emigrating European Saints begin to rise. Apostle Franklin D. Richards and his successors in the European mission were under intense pressure from members of the Church who were anxious to embark for Zion. The First Presidency added to the pressure in the Seventh General Epistle published in England in July 1852, stating, "Let all who can procure a bit of bread, and one garment on their back, be assured there is water plenty and pure by the way, and doubt no

longer, but come next year to the place of gathering, even in flocks, as doves fly to their windows before a storm."[6]

In addition to English emigrants, Scandinavian and German converts also came in increasing numbers across the trail in 1853. Danish emigrant Christian Nielsen, traveling in the sixth Mormon company of 1853 captained by John Forsgren, commented on the interaction between the English and Danish emigrants in the company.

"June 1 [1853], . . . Our Captain had requested the English emigrants that were back of us to kindly assist us in looking for the two [missing] oxen, which they did. . . .

"July 20, At 5 o'clock in the morning we journeyed . . . until we, at 11 o'clock, came to Luk Fort [Loup Fork] River. We thought that we could drive over the river, but it was too deep water for that so it was necessary that we should be ferried over; but, as we were money broke, the English emigrants paid . . . for us. . . .

"July 21, . . . One of our wagons had broke but a wheel repairer from the English company was able to put the wagon in repairs for us. . . .

"July 28, We met at this place 27 bretheren from Zion . . . that should go to Europe to perform missionary work for the church. In unison with the English emigrants . . . we finally got the bridge built upon which the English company first came over and next the 27 brethren from Zion went over the bridge. . . .

"Sept. 22, . . . [The] English emigrants carried with them the body of a certain woman that they had in one

PERPETUAL EMIGRATION FUND PROMISSORY NOTE (front and back) signed by Nancy Jane McLeave, mother of seven children, whose husband died at Bear River.

of their wagons and which they had promised another English company that they had met to take down to the valley to get buried. As we, by this time, had some empty wagons, we agreed to take the body in our wagons to have the lady buried in a graveyard with other people, which was their wish. . . .

"Sept. 29, . . . We were now on the top of the low mountains, but other wagons were still in the mountain cliff, but not together, but they had camped, waiting for assistance . . . the English company as [well as] the drivers of our company. . . . Some oxen . . . were killed and the meat divided between our companies."[7]

The year 1853 saw a fairly heavy immigration, higher than the following year, although in 1854 the numbers using the Perpetual Emigrating Fund rose and costs generally increased. Through 1854, European emigrants came by way of New Orleans, then up the Mississippi and Missouri Rivers to Keokuk, Iowa, or Mormon Grove, near Atchison, for the trip across the plains.

The 1855 emigration was altered by some specific instructions from Brigham Young. In an April 1854 letter to Franklin D. Richards, again serving as the European Mission president, Brigham wrote, "You are aware of the sickness liable to assail our unacclimated brethren on the Mississippi River; hence I wish you to ship no more to New Orleans, but ship to Philadelphia, Boston and New York."[8]

Not only was the point of arrival in the United States changed in 1855, but Brigham Young also wanted the emigrants screened carefully. Thousands of European converts had joined the Church only because they saw it as

THE MISSISSIPPI AT NEW ORLEANS. *Through 1854 Mormon emigrants came by way of New Orleans, then up the Mississippi and Missouri Rivers.*

chance to emigrate to the United States. Brigham wanted tried and true Saints to emigrate, and he wrote to Franklin D. Richards, "I will here repeat my wish and counsel to you, that in your elections of the Saints who shall be aided by the Fund, those who have proven themselves by long continuance in the Church shall be helped first, whether they can raise any means of their own or not; let those be brought, so long as you can act within the means of the Company, if they have not a sixpence in the world, but be wary of assisting any of those who come into the Church now, during these troublesome times for Britain, whose chief aim and intention may be to get to America."[9]

Highlights from the journal of 1855 emigrant Jane Hindley describe a typical journey on the "new route" from the Eastern United States:

"In the year 1855 February 16 I together with a younger Sister left home and Sailed on Board the Monas Queen for Liverpool and arrived thear Next day for the purpose of going to America, very Much against my Father's wishes. But I belived in the princaple of the gathering and felt it My Duty to go altho it was a Sever trial to Me in My feelings to leave My Native Land and the pleasing assoctiones that I had formed there but my heart was fixed. I knew in whom I had trusted and with the fire of Isrels God burning in My bosom I forsoke My home, but Not to gather wealth or the perashible things of this world. . . .

"April 24th I [left] in the train. Spent a most unpleasant night being so long in a sitting position, and [we] are still 170 miles from Pitsburge [Pittsburg, Pennsylvania]. . . .

"April 25th . . . did not see much of Pitsburg went on board the Monongahala Steam boat. . . .

"May 1st we have now arrived at a town called Louisville but could not go out. . . .

"May 6th . . . about 100 miles from St Louis . . . My feelings are very peculiar in seeing so many new places and in being so very far from Home, but feel thankfull to God for his care over us thus far and trust for the future. . . .

"May 23rd we have just arived at Mormon Grove it is a delightfull place. . . .

"June 30th we have arived at the Plat River—My face is very much burnt with the Sun.

"July 1st we have had some murmering in camp to day I was very sorry to hear it as it hurt the Captains feelings. . . .

"July 25th Helena and I went to see Chimney Rock.

"Augt 11th all well we have passed through Devils Gate.

"Sept. 3rd have arived at GSL City we went to Bro Cains House and was recived with great kindness."[10]

The 1855 European emigration that needed to use P.E.F. funds proved to be one of the largest ever, as thousands like Jane Hindley heeded the call to gather. Even under normal circumstances it would have taxed the financing of the Perpetual Emigrating Fund, but circumstances in the Utah Territory made it even worse. A severe

Far left: ON BOARD AN EMIGRANT SHIP—THE BREAKFAST BELL.
Left: AERIAL VIEW OF 1860 BOSTON. Photographer: James W. Black. In
1855 Brigham Young told his mission leaders in Europe to start using
Philadelphia, Boston, and New York as disembarking points.
Above: IOWA CITY, IOWA, 1854. "Jumping-off" point for handcart pioneers.
Photographer: Carrie Weatherby.

drought and grasshopper infestation devastated valley crops. At the end of May 1855 Heber C. Kimball recorded, "There is not fifty acres of grain in Salt Lake valley," and by the middle of June many were completely out of food.[11] From stored reserves, 40,000 pounds of flour were sent to Mormon emigrant trains on the trail.[12]

The grasshoppers came in great numbers, and Wilford Woodruff reported that the insects fell into the lake and were washed ashore in such quantities as to make a belt several rods wide varying from six to eighteen inches deep.[13] William Chandless, passing through Salt Lake City, wrote:

"If accounts be true, the drought, always feared has this year (1856) in their utmost need withered among the

people of Utah all hope of abundance; and that more terrible scourge the grasshoppers, following upon the drought, has raised a panic of actual starvation; if they should come for a succession of years, as they now have for two, a famine and a new emigration seem inevitable. The people, however, struggle bravely, dig ditches around their fields, and try to sweep the foe away; failing that, they plant crop after crop as each is eaten off, to the end of the season. Brigham Young tells the Mormons it is a judgment on them for wasting the superabundance of 1853; when much could have been stored up, but was recklessly given to animals, and almost thrown away."[14]

The economic impact of the drought and grasshopper infestation on the Mormon community stretched Church resources to the limit. It was apparent that the funds needed for immigration in 1856 would be totally inadequate. Brigham Young elected to try a plan that had been considered for years but never tried—emigration by handcart. An October 1855 epistle from the First Presidency stated,

"In regard to the foreign immigration another year [1856], let them pursue the northern route from Boston, New York, or Philadelphia, and land at Iowa city or the then terminus of the rail road; there let them be provided with hand carts on which to draw their provisions and clothing, then walk and draw them, thereby saving the immense expense every year for teams and outfit for crossing the plains.

"We are sanguine that such a train will out-travel any ox train that can be started. They should have a few good cows to furnish milk, and a few beef cattle to drive and butcher as they may need. In this way the expense, risk, loss and perplexity of teams will be obviated, and the saints will more effectually escape the scenes of distress, anguish and death which have often laid so many of our brethren and sisters in the dust."[15] The benefits listed in the epistle would prove a tragic irony in light of the subsequent suffering by the last two handcart companies of 1856.

Five handcart companies left Iowa City for the Salt Lake Valley that year. The first two companies, captained by Edmund Ellsworth and Daniel D. McArthur, made the arduous trip without major incident, both arriving in Salt Lake City on September 26. A third smaller company, captained by Edward Bunker and composed primarily of emigrants from Wales, arrived on October 2. The last two handcart companies to leave that year—the James G. Willie and Edward Martin companies—left late, while winter came early. The members of these two companies and the Hunt and Hodgett wagon trains traveling with them endured one of the most tragic journeys in all of overland emigration history.

The great Western writer Wallace Stegner described the character of typical handcart emigrants in his classic work *The Gathering of Zion*:

"In all its history, the American West never saw a

Opposite: THE HANDCART COMPANY, *C.C.A. Christensen.*
Above right: EDMUND ELLSWORTH (1819–1893)
successfully captained a handcart company to Utah in 1856.
Right: EDWARD BUNKER (1822–1901),
1856 handcart company captain.

more unlikely band of pioneers than the four hundred-odd who were camped on the bank of the Iowa River at Iowa City in early June, 1856. They were not colorful—only improbable. Looking for the brown and resolute and weather-seasoned among them, you would have seen instead starved cheeks, pale skins, bad teeth, thin chests, all the stigmata of unhealthy work and inadequate diet. There were more women than men, more children under fifteen than either. One in every ten was past fifty, the oldest a woman of seventy-eight; there were widows and widowers with six or seven children. They looked more like the population of the poor farm on a picnic than like pioneers about to cross the plains.

"Most of them, until they were herded from their crowded immigrant ship and loaded into the cars and rushed to the end of the Rock Island Line and dumped here at the brink of the West, had never pitched a tent, slept on the ground, cooked outdoors, built a campfire. They had not even the rudimentary skills that make frontiersmen. But as it turned out, they had some of the stuff that makes heroes."[16]

While most handcart companies arrived in the Salt Lake Valley with no higher mortality or difficulty than in a regular wagon company, the entire handcart effort, ten companies between 1856 and 1860, has been colored by the catastrophe of the James G. Willie and Edward Martin companies. Poor communication, inadequate supplies, lack of wood to build handcarts, and inexperienced emigrants contributed to the delay in leaving and traveling on the trail by these last two companies of 1856. Overly optimistic Church immigration agents, believing that the Lord would provide a safe journey for these two late-starting companies, allowed them to proceed, almost designing a prescription for disaster. They still might have made it, had winter not arrived early on the trail in what is present-day Wyoming.

The personal responsibility for the disaster, felt by Church leaders from Brigham Young down to the individual Church immigration agents, cannot be calculated. Some finger-pointing took place, and through the years Mormons and non-Mormons have argued about the significance of the disaster in the broader scope of Mormon history. While the circumstances that caused the tragedy are complex, nothing can erase the fact that hundreds died needlessly. To his great credit, once Brigham Young was informed that two companies were trapped in the early winter snows and in a desperate condition, he put in motion what can only be termed a heroic rescue effort. He channeled the considerable organizational skill of the Church and galvanized hundreds into action, an effort that ultimately saved the balance of the emigrants in the two handcart companies.

James G. Willie's company left Iowa City on July 15; Edward Martin's departed July 26. Almost a month later, August 11, the Willie company pulled into Florence. With the season so late, the question of proceeding was put to a vote. All but the experienced Levi Savage voted to travel. Savage, with tears running down his cheeks, reportedly pleaded for "the old, wealk [weak], and sickly to stop until another spring . . . that if such undertook the journey at that late season, of the year, that their bones would strew the way."[17] He added, "Brethren and sisters, what I have said I know to be true; but seeing you are to go forward, I will go with you, will help you all I can, will work with you, will rest with you, will suffer with you, and, if

necessary, I will die with you. May God in his mercy bless and preserve us."[18]

The Willie company left Florence on August 18, the Martin company on August 25, and the Hunt and Hodgett ox trains by September 2. John Chislett, traveling in the Willie company, later wrote, "Everything seemed to be propitious, and we moved gaily forward full of hope and faith. At our camp each evening could be heard songs of joy, merry peals of laughter, and bon mots

Opposite: MORMON EMIGRANTS BUILDING HANDCARTS, *Spiegle. Etching from Stenhouse,* Tell It All.
Right: EDWARD MARTIN *(1818–1882) and unidentified polygamous wife, c. 1857. This pioneer photographer is best known as the captain of the ill-fated 1856 Martin handcart company.*

on our condition and prospects. Brother Savage's warning was forgotten in the mirthful ease of the hour."[19]

After most of the oxen from the Hunt and Hodgett ox trains stampeded and ran off with a buffalo herd, the Willie company was compelled to remove some provisions from the wagons and place them on the handcarts. With the added burden of weight, the Willie company handcarts continued on their journey, reaching Fort Laramie in early October. Chislett recalled, "The provisions, etc., which we expected, were not there for us. Captain Willie called a meeting to take into consideration our circumstances, conditions, and prospects, and to see what could be done. It was ascertained that at our present rate of travel and consumption of flour the latter would be exhausted when we were about three hundred and fifty miles from our destination. It was resolved to reduce our allowance from one pound to three-quarters of a pound per day, and at the same time to make every effort in our power to travel faster. We continued this rate of rations from Laramie to Independence Rock."[20]

Meanwhile, Franklin D. Richards and other returning missionaries reached Salt Lake City and brought the news to Brigham Young that almost a thousand people were still on the trail, hundreds of miles from the Salt Lake Valley. While Young did not know their specific circumstances, a lifetime of trail experience whispered to him that a disaster was unfolding. His advice to the Saints at the October 1856 general conference of the Church was unequivocal:

"I will now give this people the subject and the text for the Elders who may speak to-day and during the conference, it is this, on the 5th day of October, 1856, many of our brethren and sisters are on the plains with handcarts, and probably many are now 700 miles from this place, and they must be brought here, we must send assistance to them. The text will be, 'to get them here.' I want the brethren who may speak to understand that their text is the people on the plains, and the subject matter for this community is to send for them and bring them in before winter sets in.

"That is my religion; that is the dictation of the Holy Ghost that I possess, it is to save the people. . . . This is the salvation I am now seeking for, to save our brethren that would be apt to perish, or suffer extremely, if we do not send them assistance.

"I shall call upon the Bishops this day, I shall not wait until to-morrow, nor until next day, for 60 good mule teams and 12 or 15 wagons. I do not want to send oxen, I want good horses and mules. They are in this Territory, and we must have them; also 12 tons of flour and 40 good teamsters, besides those that drive the teams. This is dividing my texts into heads; first 40 good young men who know how to drive teams, to take charge of the teams that are now managed by men, women and children, who know nothing about driving them; second, 60 or 65 good spans of mules, or horses, with harness, whipple-trees, neck-yokes, stretchers, lead chains, &c., and thirdly, 24 thousand pounds of flour, which we have on hand. . . .

"I will tell you all that your faith, religion, and profession of religion, will never save one soul of you in the celestial kingdom of our God, unless you carry out just

Opposite: HANDCART TRAIN IN A SNOWSTORM.

such principles as I am now teaching you. Go and bring in those people now on the plains, and attend strictly to those things which we call temporal, or temporal duties, otherwise your faith will be in vain; the preaching you have heard will be in vain; . . . and you will sink to hell, unless you attend to the things we tell you."[21]

Back on the Sweetwater River, the Willie company faced the beginning onslaught of successive snowstorms. They pressed on, but several times they were forced to stop, becoming snowbound. John Chislett recalled the unbelievable circumstances of the company while encamped east of Rocky Ridge just before relief arrived: "We had found a good camp among the willows, and after warming and partially drying ourselves before good fires, we ate our scanty fare, paid our usual devotions to the Deity and retired to rest with hopes of coming aid.

"In the morning the snow was over a foot deep. Our cattle strayed widely during the storm, and some of them died. But what was worse to us than all this was the fact that five persons of both sexes lay in the cold embrace of death. . . .

"It was also resolved in council that Captain Willie with one man should go in search of the supply train and apprise the leader of our condition. . . . They were absent three days—three days which I shall never forget. . . .

"The recollection of it unmans me even now—those three days! During that time I visited the sick, the widows whose husbands died in serving them, and the aged who could not help themselves, to know for myself where to

Opposite: MARTIN HANDCART COMPANY, *Clark Kelley Price.*

dispense the few articles that had been placed in my charge for distribution. Such craving hunger I never saw before, and may God in his mercy spare me the sight again. . . .

"On the evening of the third day . . . after Captain Willie's departure, just as the sun was sinking beautifully behind the distant hills, on an eminence immediately west of our camp several covered wagons, each drawn by four horses were seen coming towards us. The news ran through the camp like wildfire. . . . Shouts of joy rent the air; strong men wept till tears ran freely down their furrowed and sun-burnt cheeks, and little children partook of the joy which some of them hardly understood, and fairly danced around with gladness. Restraint was set aside in the general rejoicing, and as the brethren entered our camp the sisters fell upon them and deluged them with kisses. . . .

"That evening, for the first time in quite a period, the songs of Zion were to be heard in the camp, and peals of laughter issued from the little knots of people as they chatted around the fires. The change seemed almost miraculous, so sudden was it from grave to gay, from sorrow to gladness, from mourning to rejoicing. With the cravings of hunger satisfied, and with hearts filled with gratitude to God and our good brethren, we all united in prayer, and then retired to rest."[22]

Mary Hurren Wight, seventy years later, also recalled the arrival of the relief teams:

"Captain Willie went ahead through the snow to meet the relief wagons and get them to hurry as the people were freezing and starving to death. If help had not come when it did there would have been no one left to tell the tale. As a small girl I could hear the squeaking of the wagons as they came through the snow before I was able to see them. Tears streamed down the cheeks of the men and the children danced for joy. As soon as the people could control their feelings they all knelt down in the snow and gave thanks to God for his kindness and goodness unto them. The last supply of food in the camp had been given ou[t] two days before the relief wagons came. They came just in time to save our lives."[23]

Surviving the journey was but the beginning of Mary's trial. So frostbitten were her legs that upon her arrival in Salt Lake City the doctors told her father "that it would be necessary to amputate on[e] leg just above the knee, and the other one directly below the knee." She wrote, "M[y] father objected to this and said that his little girl had not walked for a thousand miles across the plains to have her legs cut off.

"The flesh fell away from the calves of my legs, so that it was necessary to grow new flesh. My mother put sweet-oil on my legs. I remember that on several occassions after coming to Brigham City that father walked to Ogden to secure fresh beef to [b]ind on my legs. It was three long years be fore I was able to walk."[24]

Despite the relief company's efforts, for many in the Willie company it was too late. George D. Grant, from Devil's Gate, wrote a dispatch to Brigham Young describing the situation:

"It is not of much use for me to attempt to give a description of the situation of these people, for this you will learn from your son Joseph A. and br. Garr, who are the bearers of this express; but you can imagine between five and six hundred men, women and children, worn down by drawing hand carts through snow and mud; fainting by the way side; falling, chilled by the cold; children crying, their limbs stiffened by cold, their feet bleeding and some of them bare to snow and frost. The sight is almost too much for the stoutest of us; but we go on doing all we can, not doubting nor despairing."[25]

Back on the North Platte, the Martin company fared no better. Apparently unable to pay the toll at Richard's bridge, the company forded the river, a decision that proved to be the final sacrifice for some. Josiah Rogerson later wrote:

"The crossing of the North Platte was fraught with more fatalities than any other incident of the entire journey. . . . More than a score or two of the young female members waded the stream that in places was waist deep. Blocks of mushy snow and ice had to be dodged. The result of wading of this stream by the female members was immediately followed by partial and temporary dementia from which several did not recover until the next spring."[26]

For Elizabeth Jackson, the crossing soon proved to be the greatest trial of her life:

"Some of the men carried some of the women on their back or in their arms, but others of the women tied up their skirts and waded through, like the heroines that they were, and as they had gone through many other rivers and creeks. My husband (Aaron Jackson) attempted to ford the stream. He had only gone a short distance when he reached a sandbar in the river, on which he sank

Opposite: DEVIL'S GATE, *Barna Meeker.*

down through weakness and exhaustion. My sister, Mary Horrocks Leavitt, waded through the water to his assistance. She raised him up to his feet. Shortly afterward, a man came along on horseback and conveyed him to the other side. My sister then helped me to pull my cart with my three children and other matters on it. We had scarcely crossed the river when we were visited with a tremendous storm of snow, hail, sand, and fierce winds. . . .

"About nine o'clock I retired. Bedding had become very scarce so I did not disrobe. I slept until, as it appeared to me, about midnight. I was extremely cold. The weather was bitter. I listened to hear if my husband breathed, he lay so still. I could not hear him. I became alarmed. I put my hand on his body, when to my horror I discovered that my worst fears were confirmed. My husband was dead. I called for help to the other inmates of the tent. They could render me no aid; and there was no alternative but to remain alone by the side of the corpse till morning. Oh, how the dreary hours drew their tedious length along. When daylight came, some of the male part of the company prepared the body for burial. And oh, such a burial and funeral service. They did not remove his clothing—he had but little. They wrapped him in a blanket and placed him in a pile with thirteen others who had died, and then covered him up with snow. The ground was frozen so hard that they could not dig a grave. He was left there to sleep in peace until the trump of God shall sound, and the dead in Christ shall awake and come forth in the morning of the first resurrection. We shall then again unite our hearts and lives, and eternity will furnish us with life forever more.

"I will not attempt to describe my feelings at finding myself thus left a widow with three children, under such excruciating circumstances. I cannot do it. But I believe the Recording Angel has inscribed in the archives above, and that my suffering for the Gospel's sake will be sanctified unto me for my good."[27]

Josiah Rogerson described the painful events that attended the Jackson family at the crossing:

"Aaron Jackson was found so weak and exhausted when he came to the crossing of the North Platte, October 19th that he couldn't make it and after he was carried across the ford in a wagon [I] was again detailed to wheel the dying Aaron on an empty cart with his feet dangling over the end bar to camp. After putting up his tent, I assisted his wife in laying him in his blankets. It was one of the bitter cold, black frost nights . . . and notwithstanding the hard journey the day before, I was awakened at midnight to go on guard again till six or seven in the morning.

"Putting jacket or coat on (for both sexes had for weeks past lain down at night in the clothing we had traveled in during the day) and passing out through the middle of the tent, my feet struck those of poor Aaron. They were stiff and rebounded at my accidental stumbling. Reaching my hand to his face, I found that he was dead with his exhausted wife and little ones by his side all sound asleep. The faithful and good man Aaron had pulled his last cart. . . .

"Returning to my tent from the night's guarding, I found there one of the most touching pictures of grief and bereavement in the annuls of our journey. Mrs. Jackson, apparently but just awakened from her slumber, was sitting by the side of her dead husband. Her face was suffused in tears and between her bursts of grief and wails of sorrow, she would wring her hands and tear her hair. The children blended their cries of 'Father' with that of the mother. This was love, this was affection—grief of the heart and bereavement of the soul—the like of which I have never seen since."[28]

In the ten miles from where the Martin company

consequence of the state of the weather.

We left all the uncovered Handcarts.

Tuesday 4th. Novr.
We travelled 3 Miles.

Wednesday 5th.
No travelling. Weather very severe. Sr. Mary Harper died aged 64. Our ration of flour was reduced to 4 oz. and 2 oz for the children. making 1 lb a day for the 6 of us. Through the blessing of our Father we felt as contented as when we had 1 lb per head.

Thursday 6th.
No travelling. Weather bound.

Friday 7th.
Still weather bound.

Saturday 8th.
No travelling. Weather more favourable

Sunday 9th.
We travelled 5 Miles. I have suffered very much to day with my feet, which are frost-bitten. I walked the 5 miles not wishing to burden the teams. Nearly all the Hand carts have been left behind.

Monday Novr. 10th.
We travelled 8 Miles. I rode. Our ration of flour was raised to 8 oz and 4 oz.

Tuesday 11th.
We travelled 7 Miles.

Wednesday 12th.
We travelled 6 Miles. Alfred Bloomfield Bridge died and was buried this morning. (one of 15 in one family. died by three) He was born the 25th of May 1837.

Thursday 13th.
We travelled 12 Miles. We passed Ice springs to day.

Friday 14th.
I have not been able to find out the distance travelled to day.

Saturday 15th.

forded the North Platte (near present-day Casper, Wyoming) to Red Buttes (Bessemer Bend), many company members died. At Red Buttes they became snowbound for six days, and at least fifty-six persons perished. William Binder recalled, "It became our painful duty to bury very many of our friends and traveling companions also to see our cattle vanish from our view through starvation every day."[29]

As in the case of the Willie company, relief for some in the Martin company was too late. After they left Devil's Gate with the relief teams, the weather forced them to take shelter in what many survivors called Martin's Ravine, today known as Martin's Cove. John Kirkman in one line summed up the entire experience at that place: "Death had taken a heavy toll, the ravine was like an overcrowded tomb, no mortal pen could describe the suffering."[30]

John Chislett and the rest of the Willie company reached the Salt Lake Valley about the day the Martin company left Martin's Cove. At South Pass, Chislett recalled meeting more relief teams "with several quarters of good fat beef hanging frozen on the limbs of the trees where they were encamped." He wrote, "These quarters of beef were to us the handsomest pictures we ever saw. The statues of Michael Angelo, or the paintings of the ancient masters, would have been to us nothing in comparison to these *life-giving pictures.*"[31]

It took until the end of November for the last of the two handcart and two ox-team companies to make it to the valley. The sight of the helpless victims so affected Brigham Young that he stated he would "lay an injunction and place a penalty, to be suffered by any Elder or Elders who will start the immigration across the plains after a given time; and the penalty shall be that they shall be severed from the Church."[32] He also stated, "I would give more for a dish of pudding and milk, or a baked potato and salt, were I in the situation of those persons who have just come in, than I would for all your prayers, though you were to stay here all afternoon and pray."[33]

For those in the Willie, Martin, Hunt, and Hodgett companies, was the Mormon Trail a trail of hope or a trail of death? Some would apostatize, embittered at those who sent them west so late. However, for many the trial of survival did not prove a trial of their faith. Many viewed their experience as did Elizabeth Jackson: "I believe the Recording Angel has inscribed in the archives above, and that my suffering for the Gospel's sake will be sanctified unto me for my good."[34] Many of those in the ill-fated companies simply viewed their experience on the trail as did other pioneers in years past and in years to come—as a metaphor for life.

James G. Bleak, traveling in the Martin company and one of the few who kept a daily diary, albeit brief, described his arrival in the valley in this way:

"Sunday 30th [November]

"We entered Great Salt Lake City. Elders Stevenson and S[eth] M. Blair have very kindly undertaken to provide me and my family with a home until I recover my strength and the use of my feet which are considerably frosted. For this kindness I pray God to bless them and to cause the spirit of increase to rest upon every blessing they have, and supply them with every blessing they need.

"I feel to rejoice greatly and give praise to God for my safe arrival in Zion with my wife and children after a journey of 6 months and 1 week."[35]

If Bleak's suffering failed to break his faith in a promised Zion, the trail would continue to be one of hope. No amount of suffering, not even the experiences of the Willie and Martin handcart companies, could dissuade the faithful from coming to the valley or discourage the Church from asking them to do so. In 1857 and 1858, immigration dropped significantly, but not because of the suffering on the trail in 1856. Rather, events in 1857 saw the Mormons accused of sedition against the United States,

and the Mormon Trail carried 2,500 federal troops toward Utah to put down the supposed rebellion. The old friend of the Mormons, Thomas L. Kane, brokered a peace that averted bloodshed, but it wasn't until 1859 that normal immigration resumed to the Utah Territory. In 1859 and 1860, five more handcart companies and a significant number of wagon trains followed the Mormon Trail to Zion.

By 1860, the character of all overland emigrant trails was changing. Relations with Native Americans on all the trails was deteriorating. The United States edged ever

Below left: FORT BRIDGER, Wyoming, c. 1856.
Below: THOMAS L. KANE (1822–1883),
non-Mormon friend of the Latter-day Saints.

closer to the precipice of the Civil War. The Pony Express began its short-lived mail delivery operation, followed soon by the transcontinental telegraph system. Overland stage lines brought travelers west on regular schedules. Brigham Young even entered into contracts to deliver grain to Ben Holladay's overland stage stations.

In the 1860s, the Mormon Trail would serve its last decade as a conduit for emigrants coming to Utah. The final emigration system adopted by the Church, the down-and-back Church trains, proved so efficient as to almost be forgotten in the history of the trail. ✳

THE FAITH OF JAMES G. BLEAK

~~~~~

JAMES GODSON BLEAK not only recorded his suffering in the Martin Handcart Company, but he also left a moving tribute to the power of attitude over adversity. Like others, his suffering didn't stop once he was rescued. Arriving in Salt Lake City on November 30, 1856, he couldn't walk until February 1857 because of the effects of frostbite. Through it all, his faith remained constant, as reflected in many passages in his journal, a few of which are reproduced here:

"Monday 15th [September]

"We travelled 22 miles. I began to draw the Handcart this morning but was obliged to leave it. Br. Francis Webster very Kindly persuaded me to get on his handcart and drew me 17 miles. Elder Hunter and the two sisters Brown very kindly drew me about 4 miles. For which Kindness I feel grateful, and pray God to bless them with health and strength.

"Tuesday 16th [September]

"We travelled 9 miles. Through the blessing of God I was able to draw the handcart to day, but am still very ill. . . .

"Thursday 16th [October]

"We travelled 11 miles. Our ration of flour was reduced from 1 pound to 12 oz. for adults, and from 8 oz for my children to 6 ounces a day.

"Sunday Octr 19th

"We travelled 10 Miles. We crossed the Platte, very trying in consequence of its width and the cold weather.

"Thursday 23rd Octr.

"We travelled 5 miles. For several days we have been weather bound in consequence of a heavy fall of snow.

"Friday 24th [October]

"No travelling.

"Saturday 25th [October]

"No travelling. Our rations reduced to 8 oz of flour for Adults and 4 oz for child'n.

"Sunday 26th [October]

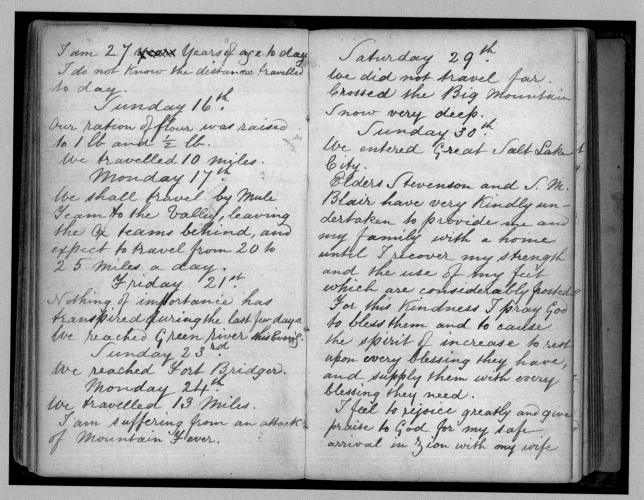

"No travelling.

"Monday 27th [October]

"No travelling.

"Tuesday 28th Octr.

"No travelling. The brethren Joseph A Young, Abel Garr and one other were met from the Valley at Red Buttes, 16 m. above Platte Bridge. 56 of our Comp'y died. When they first made their appearance I do not think there was one in Camp but shed tears of joy.

"Monday 3rd [November]

"We did not travel in consequence of the state of the weather. We left all the uncovered Handcarts.

"Wednesday 5th [November]

"No travelling. Weather very severe. Sr Mary harper died aged 64. Our ration of flour was reduced to 4 oz. and 2 oz. for the children making 1 lb a day for the 6 of us. Through the blessing of our Father we felt as contented as when we had 1 lb per head.

"Sunday 9th November

"We travelled 5 miles. I have suffered very much to day with my feet, which are frost-bitten. I walked the 5 miles not wishing to burden the teams. Nearly all the Hand carts have been left behind. Alfred Bloomfield Bridge died and was buried this morning (one of 15 in one grave side by side). He was born the 25th of May 1837.

"Monday 17th [November]

"We shall travel by Mule Team to the Valley, leaving two Ox teams behind, and expect to travel from 20 to 25 miles a day.

"Sunday 30th [November]

"We entered Great Salt Lake City. Elders Stevenson and S[eth] M. Blair have very kindly undertaken to provide me and my family with a home until I recover my strength and the use of my feet which are considerably frosted. For this kindness I pray God to bless them and to cause the spirit of increase to rest upon every blessing they have, and supply them with every blessing they need.

"I feel to rejoice greatly and give praise to God for my safe arrival in Zion with my wife and children after a journey of 6 months and 1 week.

"Thursday Janr 1st 1857

"I was taken to the fasting and prayer meeting.

"Thursday 12th [February]

"I walked to meeting for the first time this Evening, and bore my testimony to the truth of the work of the Lord.

"Saturday 4th [April]

"I left North Ogden for G. S. L. City to attend Conference . . .

"Wednesday 8th [April]

"I attended 2 meetings in the Bowery. A collection was made to raise $125 for President B. Young. As I had no cash, I gave my ring. Notice was given in the Evening that three rings had been given to the collection, and as Br. Brigham had received the amount he wanted he wished the owners of the rings to receive them back.

"Thursday 9th [April]

"I attended conference in the morning. Notice was given from the stand that there was a letter for me. I went to the stand for it. As I was receiving it President Young said to the clerk if any person applies for the one ring remaining, send them to me. I having heard what he said desired that he would keep it. He asked if it belonged to me. I said yes, that I had no cash and therefore gave my ring which I wished him to accept. He blessed me in the name of the Lord and said he had as much as he wanted then and wished me to take back my ring which I accordingly did. He asked the clerk to take my name and residence. Conference was adjourned at 12 Oclock until the 6th of next October. The letter mentioned above was from Sr. Webster."[36]

"Our Mountain Boys Went Along Full of Boldness"

DOWN-AND-BACK YEARS

IN THE SPRING OF 1860, Brigham Young's thirty-one-year-old nephew, Joseph W. Young, set out from Salt Lake City in command of an ox train with twenty-nine wagons. The train headed east to the Missouri River to pick up supplies, merchandise, and machinery. The trip was unusual only in that Young, a seasoned prairie traveler, promised to make the trip in one season—with the *same oxen* pulling the wagons. The October 10, 1860, issue of Salt Lake City's *Deseret News* reported, "On the evening of the 3d instant, Captain Joseph W. Young arrived with his freight train, consisting of some thirty wagons, with ox teams, which have made the trip to the Missouri river and back this season. The cattle, which we did not see, are said to have returned in good order and condition, looking better than some that have only been driven from the States

UTAH "MOUNTAIN BOYS," especially selected as "missionary" teamsters for Church trains, Echo Canyon, 1866. Photographer: Charles W. Carter.

this year."[1] The *Deseret News* was impressed because, until this experiment, everyone "knew" it was impossible to get the same team of oxen from Salt Lake City down to the Missouri River *and back* in one season.

Three days after his return, Joseph W. Young stood before the congregation assembled in Salt Lake City for the Church's October general conference and gave a "lecture on the science of ox-team-ology," in which he explained "the art of preserving cattle upon the plains, and making them perform two trips across the plains in one season."[2] Captain Young asserted that with careful selection and proper care of oxen, it was possible and practical to make one-season trips to and from the Missouri River. In the same meeting Brigham Young declared he "would like to have enough wagons [to] go to the frontiers to bring all the Saints who wish to come here, and it can easily be done, if the people will send back their teams . . . from this place to the Missouri river in the spring, loading up and returning in the same season."[3]

Above left: JOSEPH W. YOUNG *(1829–1873), c. 1860.*
Above right: OLD TABERNACLE AND BOWERY, TEMPLE SQUARE,
Salt Lake City, 1863. Photographer: Charles R. Savage.

Brigham Young and his counselors, who had considered discontinuing the not-so-popular handcart companies, were encouraged with the possibilities of highly organized, single-season Church-sponsored wagon trains. Such a system would answer the need for a new, efficient, low-cost system of bringing poor Saints to the Great Basin.

The general plan called for wagon trains to start from Salt Lake City in the spring loaded with food and supplies, cache these provisions at various points along the route for return use, drop off salable surplus Utah goods in the Missouri Valley, pick up Mormon emigrants and machinery, and then return to Utah. This avoided the yearly ritual of Church agents spending tens of thousands of dollars for over-priced supplies, wagons, and draft animals from profiteers at outfitting towns along the Missouri River. It also furthered Brigham Young's oft-stated plan for Mormon self-

Above left: OXEN, WAGONS, AND TEAMSTERS *AT CAMP AT THE MOUTH OF ECHO CANYON, Utah; c. 1866.*
Above right: GEORGE Q. CANNON *(1827–1901), English-born LDS Church leader and publisher, exhorted Saints to gather to Zion.*

sufficiency by using only Mormon-owned or Mormon-produced animals and supplies. Of course, increased immigration of Mormons into Utah would ensure their majority status. Indeed, nineteenth-century Mormon belief in an imminent second coming of Christ fostered an ever-increasing desire to gather with fellow Saints.

Church leaders constantly reiterated the importance of gathering. George Q. Cannon reminded the faithful that "the first duty of the Saints, after becoming associated with the work of God, is very simple, yet very important; it is to place themselves in closer connection with the work, by gathering to the place appointed. If they embrace the Gospel in London, Manchester, Glasgow or

elsewhere away from Zion . . . it is right and proper for them to gather with the Saints."[4]

After a series of highly debated planning meetings, Church leaders announced in February 1861, "Much reflection in regard to the means within our control for accomplishing certain purposes in the great work in which we are engaged . . . has induced us to present to you a plan for transporting our immigration from Florence N.T. [Nebraska] . . . and to ask your united, prompt and hearty co-operation in carrying out this plan so fraught, in our judgment, with general benefit. We are rich in cattle, but do not abound in money . . . and desire to so plan and operate as to use our small amount of money and large number of cattle in the best possible manner for accomplishing the . . . sending ox teams and loose work oxen from here to Florence to return the same season, thereby enabling us to accomplish much with comparatively a very small outlay of money."[5]

To move this plan forward, Church leaders assigned each Latter-day Saint ward (congregation) and settlement throughout the Utah Territory to donate, as they were able, a number of ox teams, wagons, teamsters, supplies, and foodstuffs. For the use of the wagon outfit, the ward was given a Church donation credit. Although some local leaders initially protested that this was too great a sacrifice for the poorer Utahns, individuals and communities

Left: THE ROUGH-AND-READY BOYS, *Black Hawk War soldiers, 1866. In the spring of 1865 a young Ute named Black Hawk led some two hundred warriors on a four-year campaign against Mormon settlers in Utah. Opposite:* JOHN R. MURDOCK *(1826–1913) captained five down-and-back companies.*

ardently pitched in by donating a great diversity and varied quantity of useful materials: clothing, tools, weapons, flour, bacon, meats, wagons, oxen, mules, horses, and a variety of other goods. The Saints donated everything from shoes to wagons. Whatever the amount, participation was widespread.

Each year the call went out in early spring to all the settlements for the needed supplies, wagons, oxen, and men. These were then collected and shipped to Salt Lake City to arrive by April.

The estimated yearly wagon-oxen-manpower statistics for the six years of "down-and-back" trips between 1861 and 1868 evidence the formidable effort made to bring poor Saints to Utah. In 1861, 200 wagons were sent east with 2,000 oxen and nearly 250 men divided into four companies. That year the trains carried 150,000 pounds of Utah flour and deposited them at four stations between the Wasatch Mountains and the Missouri River. The next year, six companies left Utah comprised of some 262 wagons, 2,880 oxen, 293 men, and 143,315 pounds of flour. The ten Church train companies of 1863 transported 236,000 pounds of flour in 384 wagons with 3,604 oxen and 488 men. In 1864, 170 wagons, 277 men, and 1,717 oxen were separated into six companies. No Church-sponsored

wagon trains were sent during 1865 because of the strain on resources during the three previous immigration years and a recent outbreak of armed battles between settlers and Indians in Utah. However, in 1866 ten ox trains were sent east with 397 wagons, 505 men, 3,043 oxen and 250,000 pounds of flour. An additional 62 wagons, 61 mules, and 50 oxen were acquired in outfitting towns in the Missouri River Valley. The increasing intensity of Utah's Black Hawk Indian War put pressure on manpower and resources, thereby causing a shutdown of Church trains in 1867. However, as in 1865, emigrants with the financial means to buy their own outfits made their way to Utah in "independent" ox teams. A massive gathering effort was made in 1868 as nearly 540 wagons, 650 men, and 4,000 oxen and mules (mules were used because of the loss of oxen during Indian conflicts) were sent out in ten companies.[6]

The Church selected seasoned individuals of proven experience and courage to captain the wagon companies. They were usually thirty to fifty years of age and held a high profile in Mormon society. For example, John Riggs Murdock, a skilled teamster with a reputation for leadership, captained five down-and-back companies. He later wrote with some justification, "I think I am safe in saying that I brought more emigrants to Utah than did any other one man. I was also most successful with my teams [oxen] and lost but very few."[7]

Each captain had a crew of at least one teamster per wagon and "an assistant [captain], a chaplain, a quartermaster, hospital steward, a camp guard, and a night guard for the stock."[8] In addition to helping coordinate the donation of supplies, local ward bishops were assigned the yearly duty of selecting men to fill these positions. They were usually unmarried men in their late teens and early twenties. No doubt most of them preferred the adventurous life on the plains to working the farm during the hot, dry months of summer. It also gave these young men a chance to be the first to meet young, unmarried female emigrants.

Referred to as the "boys," "Utah boys," "Mormon boys," or "American boys," they carried a well-earned heroic macho status with the emigrants as well as in their own communities. F. W. Blake, an English emigrant, at first complained that "the American Boys evidently have had no practice in speaking & seem deficient of thought . . . for the enlightenment of mind they are far behind the times." However, a month and a half later in the midst of Wyoming, he expressed a new-found respect, stating, "Aug[ust] 21[, 1861] . . . Had to pass some very uneven passes, which would perhaps blanch the cheek of an English Teamster to go over; but our Mountain Boys went along full of boldness & without accident."[9] In another 1861 company, Englishman George Teasdale also paid tribute: "Over we roll now on an eminence now in a vale over rough stoney ground, locking waggon wheels frequently. The boys drive well."[10]

When the down-and-back teams rolled out from the Salt Lake Valley in late April to early

Continued on page 147

Left: APPROACHING CHIMNEY ROCK, *William H. Jackson.*
Opposite: WAGONS FORDING A RIVER.

CHILDREN ON
THE TRAIL

FROM BABES-IN-ARMS to teenagers, children participated in the Mormon trek west. In many ways these young pioneers saw their experiences differently than adult counterparts saw theirs. While more likely to see the journey as an exciting adventure, children were not immune from observing and experiencing the tragedies of illness, accidents, and death.

Like adults, children five and older usually journeyed on foot rather than riding in wagons. Also, children were expected to take part in the daily chores. Younger children collected buffalo chips for campfires, picked berries, and helped with cooking. In addition to these chores, teenagers were expected to help with livestock, take care of younger siblings, and sometimes drive the oxen. The older adolescents usually took on the same tasks as adults.

Of course, emigrant children found time for fun: games, singing, enjoying stories around the campfire, playing with the few toys they brought, and exploring. In addition, the usual adolescent flirting took place.

Mary Jane Mount Tanner's reminiscence relates her 1847 experience when she crossed the plains as a ten-year-old: "There were a great many ant hills along the road raised to a considerable height where we often found beads which were, no doubt lost by the Indians and collected by those indefagitable little workers along with the gravel of which their mounds were composed. If we were

Opposite: EMIGRANTS, NEEDLE ROCKS.
Right: UNIDENTIFIED PIONEER CHILDREN.

hardy enough to risk a bite now and then we found much amusement in searching for the beads to string into neclaces. Another favorite pasttime consisted of walking far enough ahead of the train to get a little time to play; when we would drive the huge crickets . . . that abounded in some sections of the country; and build cor[r]als of sand or rocks to put them in calling them our cattle."[11]

Margaret Judd [Clawson], teenage pioneer of 1849, recorded, "After jogging along all day we camped at night. The men took care of the cattle, while the women got supper. After that was over, the young folks generally made a bon-fire and sat around it, talked, told stories, sang songs, etc."[12]

After one day's travel Margaret decided to have a reception for the other teenagers in the wagon train. "After we camped, I asked some of the girls and boys to come and spend the evening at our camp fire after their chores were done. . . . All were delighted to come. . . . In the meantime, I had asked Mother to let me make some buffalo berry pies. Of course she gave me permission. Pies were a great luxury and seldom seen on the plains. . . . My company arrived. . . . After we had chatted a while and sung some songs, I excused myself to go into the pantry (a box under the wagon) and brought out my pies. In passing the pie, I rather apologetically remarked that they might not be quite sweet enough. One gallant young man spoke up very quickly, saying, 'Oh, anything would be sweet made by those hands.' And I believed him. After serving the company, I joined them with my piece of pie. Well, the first mouthful—oh, my, it set my teeth on edge, and tasted as if it had been sweetened with citric acid! That ended my pie-making on the plains."[13]

This baby's blessing gown was sewn and embroidered by Hannah Smith as she crossed the Atlantic Ocean and trekked west in 1863. Eighty-six of her descendants were blessed in this gown.

Opposite: DOWN-AND-BACK WAGON TRAIN HEADED UP ECHO CANYON EN ROUTE EAST TO MEET MORMON EMIGRANTS AT THE MISSOURI RIVER. *Photographer: Charles W. Carter.*

Continued from page 140

May each year, they were expected to be outfitted so that each wagon had "1 tar can or keg, and at least 1 gallon of wagon grease; 2 good whip lashes. . . . For each teamster, 250 lbs. of flour, 40 lbs. of bacon, 40 lbs. of dried beef (if to be had), as much butter as each chooses and can take safely, 10 lbs. sugar, 4 lbs. coffee, 1 lb. tea, 4 quarts beans, 1 bar of soap, 4 lbs. yeast cake (or its equivalent in soda, acid or yeast powder); salt enough for teamster and team; 1 good buffalo robe and two good blankets (or their equivalent); one gallon of vinegar . . . ; 2 good pair of boots or shoes, with grease enough to keep them well greased; 3 pair of good pants, 6 shirts, 5 pairs of socks, 3 overshirts, and coats enough for comfort, with needles and thread for mending; 1 good gun (double barrelled shot gun preferable) with plenty of powder, balls and shot; one 2 gallon water can or keg."[14]

As the "boys" hit the Mormon trail eastward, they settled into the routine of their individual duties. After the captain, whose word was law, the teamster was probably the next most important position in the success of a wagon company. He needed to be confident and at ease with handling oxen. To be a teamster required the skills to prevent the always-threatening stampedes, pace the oxen to avoid fatigue, and safely guide ox and wagon over rough terrain and through water crossings. His other

Opposite: THE DOCK AT PLYMOUTH, ENGLAND, 1863.
Photographer: Charles W. Carter.
Above right: EMIGRANT SHIP, C.C.A. Christensen.

duties included the nightly check for wheel stress and the greasing of axles. Each morning brought the yoking and hitching of the usually reluctant and uncooperative cattle.

The "night guards for the stock" gathered the oxen into a corral each morning after a dusk-to-dawn vigil over the grazing and sleeping animals. During the day, these guards (usually a half-dozen per company) attempted to sleep in the supply-filled, hurky-jerky wagons.

Among the other responsibilities performed by the team were the quarter-mastering of supplies, mess duties, scouting for danger, and maintaining the spiritual well-being of team members. This pattern continued throughout the down-and-back years.

However, all was not work, as Captain Murdock admitted: "It generally took about nine weeks to cross the plains, and though it was a laborious trip, we had a great deal of enjoyment out of it. We had musicians with their instruments and would sometimes have what the boys called 'stag dances,' as there were no ladies with us on the 'down' trip. There were always several trains on the road which frequently camped close to ours, so the drivers often mingled with each other and engaged in such contests as wrestling, racing, and jumping. I took a great deal of pleasure in such association with the boys."[15]

Early in May 1861, after the wagon trains had

departed, news came from the East that the "Civil war has as at length been inaugurated in the United States by the attack upon Fort Sumter in the harbor of Charleston, South Carolina, by the Carolinians."[16] The down-and-back plan proved fortuitous to Mormon immigration as supplies and draft animals were soon in short (and expensive) supply during the Civil War.

While the Utah boys headed east, Church agents and

emigrants in Europe busily prepared for the ocean voyage to the United States to meet the "down" wagon trains. The Church train system took an incredible degree of planning and organizing to time the arrival of teamsters with U.S. and European emigrants at the outfitting town. Success of the down-and-back trains hinged entirely on the timing.

During the winter, Church immigration agents chartered sailing ships, purchased supplies for the ocean voyage, and enlisted Mormon emigrants. In the spring, LDS leaders supervised the boarding of vessels, organized the emigrants into groups, and chose voyage leaders—all in preparation for departure to America.

European emigrants funneled into Liverpool (and occasionally London) from Germany and Scandinavia to join British Latter-day Saints for staggered departures starting in mid-April and continuing until the end of May. Other ships left from port cities on the continent. The Atlantic voyage to New York City's Castle Garden emigrant station lasted from four to eight weeks.

For many, leaving for their new American Zion meant never seeing family and friends again. Englishman Frederick Weight recalled his departure from his family: "I shall never forget the night when my father wished me goodbye. He was just going up to bed and he had to go to his work early and would not see me again. That was the last time I ever saw him."[17] William Wood's worried non-Mormon parents voiced their kind good-byes "but expressed their sorrow that [he was] led away by such a 'disrespectable' people as the Mormons."[18] Other emigrants voyaged to Utah as a family—some even as extended families.

In 1863, noted British author Charles Dickens visited the London docks to witness Latter-day Saints preparing to depart on the ship *Amazon*. He wrote, "My Emigrant Ship lies broadside on to the wharf. Two great gangways . . . connect her with the wharf; and up and down these gangways, perpetually crowding to and fro and in and out, like ants, are the Emigrants. . . . Some with cabbages, some with loaves of bread, some with cheese and butter, some with milk and beer, some with boxes, beds, and bundles, some with babies—nearly all with children. . . . To and fro, up and down, aboard and ashore. . . . Now I have seen Emigrant ships before . . . and these people are so strikingly different from all other people in like circumstances whom I have ever seen, that I wonder aloud, 'What would a stranger suppose these emigrants to be!' The weather-browned captain of the 'Amazon' . . . says 'What indeed! The most of these came aboard yesterday evening. They came from various parts of England in parties that had never seen one another before. Yet they had not been a couple of hours on board, when they established their own police, made their own regulations, and set their own watch at all the hatchways. Before nine o'clock the ship was as orderly and quiet as a man-of-war.'"[19]

Twenty-five-year-old emigrant James Linford left Liverpool aboard the ship *Manchester* on April 16, 1861, "with 380 passengers [who came from Britain, Denmark, Sweden, Norway, and Switzerland]. . . . It was not a passenger ship and did not have any conveniences for our comfort. The ship's second deck was divided into two compartments, one for the married folks and single girls, and one for the single men. We named our compartment Bachelor's Hall. The berths were built of rough lumber, and the passengers furnished their own bedding or went without. . . . We arrived in New York, May 18 [15], 1861; . . . we had to pass before the doctors for them to decide whether or not we were fit subjects to land."[20]

The emigrant ship *Franklin* left Hamburg, Germany, on April 14, 1862. Jens Weibye stated, "I was appointed to locate the emigrants in their bunks. . . . These bunks (160 in number) were so wide that three persons could easily have room in one of them side by side. After getting our baggage in order, we received our rations . . . ; these consisted of beef, pork, peas, beans, potatoes, pearl barley, rice, prunes, syrup, vinegar, pepper, coffee, tea, sugar, butter, rye bread, sea biscuits, water, flour, salted herring, salt and oil (for the lamps)." Unfortunately, "some of the emigrants carried the

measles with them from home and the disease soon spread to all parts of the ship, so that no less than forty persons, mostly children, were attacked at once." Three adults and forty-three children out of the 413 emigrating Saints died on this voyage. Despite this tragedy, emigrants tried to enjoy life as "most every day we amused ourselves a short time by dancing on the deck to music played by some of our brethren or members of the crew."[21]

Much more common than measles was an ailment that often strikes those not used to sea travel. William

Opposite: THE PORT OF NEW YORK, *showing emigrants' entryway into America (Castle Garden is the round building).* *Right:* NEBRASKA CITY, RIVER FRONT FROM THE IOWA SIDE, 1865, *Alfred Mathews.*

Wood reported of his 1862 voyage, "After the ship had got fairly out to sea the people were laying in all directions with sea-sickness. It was a severe trial to them."[22]

Once in New York, the immigrants faced new challenges in preparing for the trip to the Midwest. They had to be aware of deceptive merchants, as Linford found out: "Those who had money went to the stores in New York to buy food for the journey on the train to St. Joseph, Missouri. The dealers would ask six pence for six cents worth of goods thus doubling their profits. They tried the trick on me, but when they asked six pence for an article, I asked them if they did not mean six cents. They wanted to know how long I had been in the country, when I told them they appeared not to believe me. I had learned the relative value of money . . . by conducting the [Mormon] Elders to the money brokers in Liverpool to exchange their American coin for English money."[23]

In 1861 it took ten days to travel from New York to Florence, Nebraska. To get there, the Mormon emigrants first traveled by chartered railway cars to St. Joseph, Missouri, and then by riverboat up the Mississippi and Missouri Rivers to Florence, which remained the Saints' outfitting location until 1864. From 1864 through 1866 Wyoming, Nebraska, became the outfitting town. By 1867, west-moving railroad construction allowed North Platte (some 300 miles from Omaha) in south-central Nebraska to be the village where emigrants set out in wagons. In 1868, with railroad construction quickly moving westward, the "jumping-off" spot for Mormons soon moved from Laramie, Wyoming to Benton.

As emigrants began arriving at the outfitting stations from May to July, they found a beehive of activity. Church agents had set up camps, warehouses, supply stores, corrals, and weighing machines. Those with the financial wherewithal were assisted in buying their own wagons and outfits and were formed into so-called independent companies.

Poor Saints reported to the Church agent in charge of down-and-back trains. When James Linford arrived in Florence, he reported, "We camped in the deserted houses

of the early pioneers; it being the place where many of the exiles from Nauvoo wintered [Florence was formerly called Winter Quarters]. . . . While waiting for the [wagon] train of Captain Ira Eldridge to start for Utah, my companion William Clayson and I walked to Omaha to seek work for a few days; he found work at his trade of slipper making, and I at repairing shoes. . . . After staying in Florence . . . I commenced my journey across the plains on June 30, 1861, in Captain Ira Eldridge's Company. I was appointed captain of the wagon and my duties were to draw the provisions and keep peace in our little company [540 members]; in this I got along very well with all except one family. They were always grumbling about the food, saying among other things, that they could not get enough to eat. The mother had the misfortune to fall under the wagon and was severely injured."[24]

By the 1860s there were many readily available published accounts, in the U.S. and abroad, about the overland wagon journey from the Missouri River to the western United States. No doubt many of these European and American Mormon emigrants read of the trials, characters, mishaps, sights, and sounds of trail life. However, reading was one thing, while actually experiencing it was another. None of these newcomers had weathered the blazing heat of Nebraska's flatlands or the eerie lonesomeness of Wyoming's windy, hot

days and chilly nights; few had traveled dangerous mountain passes, or ferried and forded swollen streams and rivers one day, only to hope to find water a few days later. Certainly none had walked fifteen to twenty-five rough miles each day for ten to twelve weeks. Braving rattlesnakes and buffalo-caused stampedes would be new. Undoubtedly they had heard stories of hostile Indians, even though most migrants traveled without incident. Like emigrants in previous years, sickness, death, and mishap nagged at their

Opposite: IRA ELDREDGE *(1810–1866), down-and-back captain.*
Right: OMAHA, NEBRASKA, AUGUST, 1865.

heels, as did the constant rumors of the misfortunes befalling other travelers. The experience proved unlike anything these pioneers had ever known in their cities, villages, and farms of Germany, England, Scandinavia, France, and the eastern United States.

Fortunately, these tenderfoot emigrants traveled in well-supplied companies under the guidance of tough, practical captains and teamsters. James Linford blandly stated that "the interests of the emigrating Saints on the railroad, the steam boat, and by ox teams were looked after by competent men."[25] On the other side of the coin, captain John Murdock wrote of his new charges, "It was certainly novel to see a train starting out with everything that could be put into wagons and everything that could be tied to the outside, such as buckets, cans and all kinds of cooking utensils. It reminded one of an old turkey with a brood of young ones keeping her company."[26]

As the companies, varying in size from 70 to 700 individuals, began their journey, they soon established a routine that would be their daily pattern through Nebraska, Wyoming, and finally into Salt Lake City: "The company was called together morning and evening for prayers. In forming camp after the days journey, the wagons were drawn into a circle to form a corral. When the cattle were unyoked, they were given into the care of the herders who took them to the feed which was located by the captain of the guard. There were men appointed every night to guard the camp; this guard was composed of emigrants, while the cattle guard was made up of men [from] Utah.
. . . Toward the evening the company would gather buffalo chips with which to cook supper and to make a light. After breakfast and prayers the captain would call out, 'Gather up the cattle.' They were run into the corral to be yoked up; when all was ready to start, only one wagon at a time would leave the circle, no one trying to get ahead or out of his place."[27]

Left: MORMON TRAIL ENCAMPMENT, 1866.
Photographer: Charles R. Savage.
Right: PIONEERS FORDING THE PLATTE RIVER, c. 1866.

Whereas the pioneering wagon trains and handcarts of previous decades averaged between nine to fifteen miles per day, the experienced teamsters of the down-and-back companies could make an impressive twenty miles a day. During their long day, wagon companies took three to four planned breaks to check and maintain wagon axles and wheels and to conserve animal and human strength: a short midmorning break to rest, water, and check draft

animals; the two-hour "nooning" break that allowed emigrants to rest, eat, and unyoke and graze the oxen; and a short afternoon and then an additional late afternoon break that repeated the needs of the morning break. Rather than a luxury, these breaks were a necessity for long-haul travel. Emigrants who foolishly pushed too hard ultimately paid the price with crippled or dead animals,

broken equipment, and their own exhaustion—a dangerous combination in the harsh western terrain.

Unfortunately, dangers, tragedies, and mishaps were a part of the trek west, even in the 1860s. Twenty-five-year-old teamster Orley Bliss recorded on July 10, 1864, "A child died last night and a little boy strayed away." Fortunately, the lost boy was found the next evening.[28]

While some companies traveled without any problems from local Indian tribes, hostilities occasionally proved a very real concern. Independent company member Peter Nielsen wrote, "Driving the loose Stock & our teams up a Ravin[e] to a Watering Place about 3/4 of a mile or more from Camp the I[n]dians came upon us from their Hiding Place. 7 of our Company war badly wounded[.] John Svenson came to Camp with 2 Arrows in his left Arm. Peter 'Doctor' one Arrow in his Cheek & one clear through his neck. a swedish Bro[ther] had one Arrow in the small of his Back. he never was able to walk on the Journey. . . . [W]e relieved them all but Peter Doctor the one through his neck would not come out. . . . [W]e laid the Doctor on

Above: SIOUX INDIAN VILLAGE, *Platte River.*
Photographer: Bierstadt Bros.
Opposite: WAGON TRAIN, UTAH, *c. 1867.*
Photographer: Charles W. Carter.

the Ground with his Haed resting on a Ox Yoke two men sitting on him. Albert Davis with one strong Pull manage[d] to pull out the Arrow. Bro. Holmgreen . . . was shot by a Bullet. he fell arrose again and staggered 3–4 Steps and fell again we took him for dead. Andersen was shot by Bullet it took a litle bit off his Cheek & a litle bit off his nose him & Holmgreen laid like the[y] were daed until we had cared for the others wounds."[29]

While Indian attacks were the exception, other dangers were not. Teamsters worked hard, and their efforts occasionally put them in harm's way. Teamster Zebulon Jacobs good-humoredly wrote in his journal, "[July] 19th, went 9 miles and came to and crossed the Loup Fork Ferry, got over all right. I had the pleasure of getting dunked several times while helping the waggons over, was more hungry with a small amount of tired." Particularly dangerous was the night "the mules and horses took a notion they would go . . . , started in persute it was so dark that we had to wate for the lightning to tell which way we were going. saw something moving in the distance for an instant started in chase. . . . wated for another flash, head[ed] then in a swamp but did not know the swamp was there followed [until] I found myself . . . deep in mud and water and came to the pius conclusion to go to camp and wate till morning after many tumblings and getting's up."[30]

SAVAGE & OTTINGER   SALT LAKE CITY.

Left: PIONEER BURIAL AT WOLF CREEK, *July 25, 1861, George M. Ottinger. The burial of John Morse on the night of July 25, 1861, on the plains of Nebraska.*
Right: GEORGE TEASDALE *(1831–1907), 1861 English emigrant, became an apostle twenty-one years later. Photographer: Charles R. Savage.*

Despite all the work and danger, the emigrants and teamsters managed to have more than a little fun. In the evenings "the emigrants often had a concert or dance by the light of their campfire."[31] There were fireside stories, occasional social visits and games between companies, and hunting, fishing, and climbing. Romance and flirting did not take a break for wagon travel, as Orley Bliss noticed: "[July 9,] at camp sparking is extensive this evening. . . . [July 19,] at camp it rained this afternoon. the boys and girls are heavy on the spark this evening."[32]

The teamsters could not pass up the chance for practical jokes. Nineteen-year-old Zebulon Jacobs wrote that on the morning of August 17, 1861, "Waked up and all hands that were in the tent began laughing at each others faces. Come to find out we had all of our faces be-smeared with tar and waggon griese, some of the boys from the other camp paid us a visit and left their compliments upon our faces." Sometimes the "Utah boys" also had fun at the expense of the greenhorn emigrants, as Jacobs reports: "[August 24] Parker and myself went on guard about 10 saw a man coming towards us hailed him the 2nd time no stop so we stoped him, and . . . found that he belonged to H.P. Kimball train which was a short distance a head. the boys had got him to catch rabits yankee fashion

back to his train . . . then went to roost."[33]

After about two and a half months on the trail, the wagon trains arrived in Salt Lake City at intervals in August, September, and October. George Teasdale summed up his last day of westward adventure in his journal: "Friday 27th Sep. An early rise for this day we were obliged to double teams and it was resolved for us to roll into the city we started at 1/2 past 7 crossed the lit[t]le mountain rolled on 12 miles and camped on the square in Salt Lake City and here we have arrived at our destination all the excitement of the journey is over. We have been very much blessed for there has been but very little mortality when we consider our company 54 waggons and near 200 souls but 3 deaths 1 man drowned accidently 1 woman and a child amongst the cattle we have lost about 26 head of stock but we had a large herd. We have been favoured with very fine weather let all the glory be to *him* who has so highly favoured us. And now Cap. Sixtus E. Johnson adie[u]. I shall not easily forget the pleasant times and conversations I have had in taking the days journeys and enjoying the chat that frequently followed the minutes of the previous days journey."[34]

by building a small fire, lying down by it with an open sack for the rabits to run and the[n] hit them on the head with a club now and then giving a low whistle. the boys going out round to drive them in. when all of a suden the boys gave a yell the man thought that the Indians were upon him and off he started at full run he had run about a mile when we stoped him the fellow was scared out of his wits, the cause was that he knew every thing but yankee tricks, took him

Brigham Henry [Harry] Roberts, who trekked west at age ten with his sixteen-year-old sister, remembered his companies' arrival in Salt Lake City: "People had turned out to welcome the plains-worn emigrants and were standing on the street sides to greet them. Some horsemen dashed up the street swinging their cowboy hats. . . . Along the road, perhaps nearly halfway from the mouth of Parley's Canyon to the city . . . I saw a bright-colored, dainty, charming little girl approaching me in the middle of the street. . . . Three months' journey over the plains and through the mountains without hat or coat or shoes for most of the way had wrought havoc with my appearance. My hair stuck out in all directions; the freckles seemed deeper and more plentiful and the features less attractive than when the journey began. Shirt and trousers barely clung to my sturdy form, and my feet were black and cracked but now covered by the shoes I had taken from the feet of a dead man at a burnt station. These I was wearing in compliment to my entrance into 'Zion.' . . . She had on her arm a basket of luscious fruit, peaches, plums, and grapes. These she extended to me. . . . As soon as I had obtained what I supposed a reasonable portion, I wondered how I could get this fruit so wonderful back to Mary. . . . I finally turned back as best I could to the wagon where Mary was concealed under the wagon cover because of her being a little ashamed of her appearance. Running behind the wheel ox and climbing up on the tongue of the wagon, I called to my sister, handed to her the fruit, and then scrambled back to the ground and ran for my place at the head of the train and marched on until the head of Main Street was reached."[35]

Some emigrants were lucky enough to have family, friends, or acquaintances awaiting their arrival. Young Brigham [Harry] Roberts's mother had preceded her son and daughter to Utah. Upon arriving in downtown Salt Lake City, Roberts noticed that "by and by there were numerous meetings in various groups of people, friends of the emigrants, parents, and sweethearts, and perhaps in some instances wives of the teamsters that had returned. There seemed to be an air of cheerfulness." However, young Harry and Mary could not find their mother. "The spirit of sadness, if it was not forlornness, settled upon me," he wrote. "Presently, however, approaching from the

Below: Salt Lake Tabernacle during construction, 1866. Right: Brigham Henry Roberts (1857–1933), who emigrated from England as a child in 1866.

west gate [of Temple Square], I saw a woman in a red and white plaid shawl slowly moving. . . . She seemed to be daintily picking her way. . . . The woman was moving in my direction, and the closer she came the stronger the conviction grew upon me that there was my mother. I would have known her from the dainty cleanliness of everything about her. I stood until she came nearly parallel to where I sat; then sliding from the tongue of the wagon, I said, 'Hey Mother,' and she looked down upon my upturned face. Without moving she gazed upon me for some time and at last said, 'Is this you, Harry? Where is Mary?'"[36]

Other newly arrived emigrants camped out in their wagons until accommodations and work could be provided, usually by a bishop assigned the task of helping them. The trains were now disbanded. Borrowed teams, wagons, and equipment were returned to their owners. Finally, the steadfast Utah boys went home filled with stories to share. On October 8, 1864, four days after completing the down-and-back round trip, teamster Orley Bliss recorded that he "hunted cattle went to the [Salt Lake] Theatre this evening."[37] Two days later he was on his way home to Toquerville in southern Utah.

The down-and-back system proved very successful in a variety of ways. It brought in great numbers of emigrants in a relatively safe, economical, and timely manner. More than 2,500 men guiding an estimated 2,000 wagons pulled by some 17,500 oxen, mules, and horses helped transport approximately 16,000 of the 20,000 emigrants who made their way to Zion between 1861 and 1868.[38] An era was ending as the last Church-organized wagon

THE RAILROAD REACHES THE 100TH MERIDIAN.

train entered Salt Lake City in the fall of 1868, while the new era of the "iron horse" was about to dawn on the horizon of the next year's spring. ✳

DANCING, FISHING, AND SPARKIN'

HEAVY PHYSICAL TOIL, mind-numbing heat, fear-inducing storms, a plodding pace, unanticipated mishaps, and the ever-present reminders of potential danger and tragedy proved to be the lot of westward journeying pioneers. Many of these emigrants attempted to balance the difficulties and tragedies by singing and "visiting" while walking, and, when the opportunity presented itself, by hunting; fishing; stargazing; dancing; exploring and climbing; writing their names on landmarks; visiting nearby emigrant camps; sharing yarns and reciting poetry around the campfire; participating in concerts, parties, games, and races (on foot and on horseback); celebrating the Fourth and Twenty-fourth of July; and "sparkin'" (flirting, usually by the young folks).

Sixtus E. Johnson, captain of an 1861 wagon company, recalled "some evenings after supper a violin was brought out and the time was spent in singing and dancing until the bugles sounded for the people to retire."[39] Fredrick Weight, who crossed the plains in 1852, also reported, "Sometimes we had a little dance in the evenings when all things went well and this was the first place I ever saw a Cottillion danced in all my life. I soon learned to dance them and some other dances also."[40]

Independence Rock was a particular goal for westward emigrants. Upon arrival, the travelers usually took the time to carve their names into the rock. Traveling with her parents in Brigham Young's 1848 company, twelve-year-old Rachel Woolley wrote, "We heard so much of Independence Rock long before we got there. . . . Father staid long enough for us children to go all over it. . . . It is an immense rock with holes and crevices where the water is dripping cool and sparkling. We saw a great many names of persons that had been cut in the rock."[41] Another 1848 pioneer, Curtis Edwin Bolton, wrote that while his company "camped there, the band played most beautifully til late. Some danced up on top of the rock where the band were. It was a clear night and full moon."[42]

Remembering his trip across the plains as a ten-year-old in 1848, Samuel H. Smith wrote, "as we travelled up the Platte I often amused myself by fishing and by many other objects that was quite new and interesting."[43] However, fishing was not just for the young. Near Fort Bridger, Wyoming, young-at-heart Church leader Wilford Woodruff recorded in his diary: "As soon as I got my breakfast I riged up my trout rod that I had brought with me from Liverpool, fixed my reel, line, & Artificial fly & went to one of the brooks close by Camp. . . . I went & flung my fly onto the [water] And it being the first time that I ever tried the Artificial fly in America, or ever saw it tried, I watched it as it floated upon the water with as much intens interest As Franklin did his kite when he tried to draw lightning from the skies. And as recieved great Joy when he saw electricity . . . descend on his kite string in like manner was I highly gratified when I saw the nimble trout dart my fly hook himself & run away with the line but I soon worried him out & drew him to shore & I fished two or three hours including morning & evening & I cought twelve in all."[44]

Many young adults met, flirted, and courted on the trail. Some actually married while still en route west; others waited until they reached the Salt Lake Valley.

Twenty-year-old 1848 emigrant Aroet Hale stated that while the journey "was hard on Old People and Woman with Chraldren The Young folks had injoyment." He wrote, "Presedent Young and Kimble was Verry kind and indulgent to the Young. [The wagon companies] frequently Stop within a Mile or So apart. The Young [w]ould Viset from One Camp to the Other. and frequently would get musick and have a good Dance on the Ground. . . . I formed an acuantance with a Youn[g] Lady Crosing the Plains that I after wards Marr[i]ed. her Name was Olive Whittle . . . from Canada. So I done My Sparking along the road. So I did not have So much to Do after I got into the Valley."[45]

Acts of heroism sometimes sparked romantic interest. Lydia Ann Lake Nelson recalled how, as an eighteen-year-old in 1850, she witnessed "the most vivid event of the journey." She continued, "In crossing the [Green] river the wagon box floated off a wagon . . . and began drifting downstream. In the box were a young woman named Snyder and a little girl about nine years old. . . . The only man in the company who dared to swim the stream and effect a rescue was a youth named Price W. Nelson, a young man who at the time I had paid no attention to. He was of quiet nature and I knew nothing of him except that he drove his aunt's team. After this we two became better acquainted which resulted in our marriage after arriving in Salt Lake City."[46]

AMERICAN FORK [UTAH] BRASS BAND, 1866.

Some couples were not "allowed" to wait for marriage. Abner Blackburn reported in 1847, while in the midst of the Wyoming wilderness, "There was a coupple of young folks in the company spooning and licking each other ever since we started on the road. The whole company were tired of it and they were persuaded to marry now and have done with it and not wait until their journeys end. The next evening we had a wedding . . . and after come the supper with the best the plains could furnish. Then came the dance or howe down. The banjo and the violin made us forget the hardships of the plains."[47]

An Epilogue

THE END OF THE TRAIL

ON MAY 10, 1869, a Utah broadside proclaimed, "At Noon to-day, in the vicinity of the Northern shores of the Great Salt Lake, the Last Rail will be laid on the Great Iron Way that spans from ocean to ocean the American Continent. This grand triumph of American skill and enterprise is an event of which the Nation may well be proud. It is unequalled in the annals of railroad building, and as a work of enterprise and energy it stands unrivalled in the World. When the last spike shall have been driven, the electric wire will flash the joyous news to the four quarters of the Globe. . . . The benefits that will accrue to our country and the world at large by the completion of the Union and Central Pacific Railroads can scarcely be grasped by the most astute intellects of the age, so vast, so stupendous will they be. Upon the bosom of this National High Way will be conveyed the commerce of many nations."[1]

These laudatory declarations proved true, for the railroad changed the face of the West. It provided easy access for ever-increasing numbers of people wishing to visit, conduct business, or settle "out west." An 1869 Union Pacific poster grasped the changes as it invited "Travelers for Pleasure, Health or Business" to enjoy "luxurious cars," promising they would "find a Trip over The Rocky Mountains Healthy and Pleasant." It also alerted "gold, silver and other miners," "Now is the time to seek your Fortunes in Nebraska, Wyoming, Arizona, Washington, Dakotah, Colorado, Utah, Oregon, Montana, New Mexico, Idaho, Nevada or California."[2] Indeed, the railroad proved a vital factor in the continuing settlement of the West.

In fact, the joining of the transcontinental railroad on May 10, 1869, at Promontory, Utah, brought an end to the era of Mormon immigration by wagon train. The vanguard wagon trek of 1847 from the Missouri River to

Opposite: UNION PACIFIC RAILROAD POSTER *announcing the beginning of railway service from the Atlantic to the Pacific.*

Above: MORNING BEFORE LAYING THE LAST RAIL, Promontory, Utah, May, 1869.

Utah took *four months.* An 1869 transcontinental railway trip took only *eight days.*

The Mormons took advantage of the newly completed railroad and the advent of steamships to aid their immigration. On June 2, 1869, a company of Saints left Liverpool, England; twenty-four days later Salt Lake City's *Deseret News* reported, "The first fruits of this year's immigration from Europe reached Ogden [Utah] last evening

at five o'clock. They left Liverpool on the steamship *Minnesota* on the 2nd instant, under the charge of Elder Elias Morris, late president of the Welsh district, the greater part of the company being from the Welsh Principality. A little more than three weeks has brought them the whole distance of the weary way that once took the best part of the year to travel. This being the first company which has come all the way across the continent from the Atlantic to Utah on the Great Highway, their journey will long be remembered as inaugurating an epoch in our history. Early this morning the greater portion of the immigrants had found homes, numbers leaving to settle in the northern counties of the Territory."[3]

LDS emigrant companies would continue to bring Saints to the Great Basin via steamship and railroad well into the first decade of the twentieth century, at a rate of approximately two thousand per year. For more than six decades this new American religion advocated gathering to one place, first in Ohio, then in Missouri, followed by Illinois and finally Utah. However, by the mid-1890s some Church leaders began encouraging members to stay in their homelands. In 1895 Apostle Francis M.

Opposite: JOINING OF THE UNION PACIFIC AND THE CENTRAL PACIFIC RAILROADS, *Promontory, Utah, May 10, 1869. Photographer: Andrew J. Russell.*
Above right: INDIANS IN FRONT OF ZION'S COOPERATIVE MERCANTILE INSTITUTION, *Main Street, Salt Lake City, 1869. Photographer: Charles W. Carter.*
Right: LOOKING SOUTH ALONG MAIN STREET, *Salt Lake City, 1869.*

Lyman stated, "The spirit of this work [Mormonism] gathers the people. We never took up an argument with the people to convince them that they need to come here. Why, in many instances we have to try and quiet their nerves and keep them from gathering, in order that the Church abroad may be strong enough to sustain the Elders in the missionary field. I have thought we have depleted our missions more than we ought to have done. I am not questioning my brethren who preside over me and have directed these affairs; but these have been the sentiments of my heart, that we have allowed the people to gather more rapidly than was wise in view of the desire to spread [abroad] the principles of eternal truth in the world."[4] Fifteen and a half years later in February 1911, Church President Joseph F. Smith (nephew of founder Joseph Smith) and his counselors officially advised the British

Saints, "The establishment of the latter-day Zion on the American continent occasions the gathering of the Saints from all nations. This is not compulsory, and particularly under present conditions, is not urged, because it is desirable that our people shall remain in their native lands and form congregations of a permanent character."[5]

Somehow, post-1869 Mormon emigrants were never considered "pioneers." It was a title awarded only to those who journeyed on the rough wagon and handcart trails to Zion between 1846–1869. The honoring of pioneers began within a few short years after the arrival of the first Latter-day Saints into the Salt Lake Valley. Yearly Twenty-fourth of July celebrations, written and oral reminiscences and histories, ever-remindful laudatory speeches, and pioneer associations and museums joined to etch into the minds of Mormons of all ages the important example and role played by the trail pioneers. In 1896, eighty-nine-year-old Church President Wilford Woodruff, a pioneer of 1847, stood at the pulpit in the Salt Lake Tabernacle and told his Saints, "I heard the Prophet Joseph [Smith]

bear his testimony. . . . I have lived to see the words of the Prophet of God being fulfilled concerning Zion, concerning the mountains of Israel, and the gathering together of the Lord's people to prepare for the coming of the Son of Man. We have been led to these mountains."[6]

Early on, Brigham Young, as only he could, painted this verbal tribute to the Mormon vanguard pioneers of 1847: "We made and broke the road from Nauvoo to this place. Some of the time we followed Indian trails, some of the time we ran by the compass; when we left the

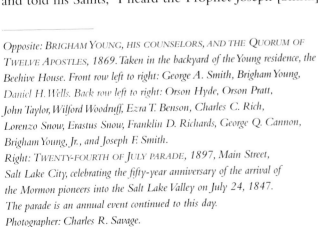

Opposite: BRIGHAM YOUNG, HIS COUNSELORS, AND THE QUORUM OF TWELVE APOSTLES, *1869. Taken in the backyard of the Young residence, the Beehive House. Front row left to right: George A. Smith, Brigham Young, Daniel H. Wells. Back row left to right: Orson Hyde, Orson Pratt, John Taylor, Wilford Woodruff, Ezra T. Benson, Charles C. Rich, Lorenzo Snow, Erastus Snow, Franklin D. Richards, George Q. Cannon, Brigham Young, Jr., and Joseph F. Smith.*
Right: TWENTY-FOURTH OF JULY PARADE, *1897, Main Street, Salt Lake City, celebrating the fifty-year anniversary of the arrival of the Mormon pioneers into the Salt Lake Valley on July 24, 1847. The parade is an annual event continued to this day.*
Photographer: Charles R. Savage.

Missouri river we followed the Platte. And we killed rattlesnakes by the cord . . . and made roads and built bridges till our backs ached. Where we could not build bridges . . . we ferried our people across. . . . For some 1200 or 1300 miles we carried every particle of provision we had when we arrived here. . . . Helter skelter, topsy turvy, with broken down horses, ring-boned, spavined, pole evil, fistula and hipped; oxen with three legs, and cows with one teat. This was our only means of transportation, and if we had not brought our goods in this manner we would not have had them, for there was nothing here. You may say this is a burlesque. Well, I mean it as such, for we, comparatively speaking, really came here naked and barefoot."[7]

The trail took lives and gave lives. On the extremes, it was high adventure for some while low despair for others. Yet the trail provided a commonly held purpose as well as faith and hope for a new and better life in the Mormon Zion. It was a means of gathering a religious society. For some the trail began in New York with their prophet Joseph Smith, and for others it began at the docks of Liverpool. Whether it was the exodus from Nauvoo or the subsequent gathering from the outfitting points at Florence, Iowa City, or Wyoming, Nebraska, the true Mormon Trail was not on the plains but in the spirit and heart of the people—individually and as a group.

Perhaps 1849 pioneer Lucy Meserve Smith spoke for many Mormon emigrants when she likened her arrival in the Salt Lake Valley to reaching the promised land in the afterlife: "Oct. 27th., We got into Salt Lake City about 11 o'clock P.M., tired and hungry, but I must cook supper for myself and the teamsters then I could go back to my wagon and go to bed thanking our heavenly father for our safe arrival. We found my husband's father and mother, brother and wife and sisters, all well and pleased to greet us. They made a feast next day had us all to partake with them. It was a great treat to sit at the table with long absent relatives and friends. I feel that it is a foretaste of the resurrection of the just."[8] ✳

Left: Mormon Church president WILFORD WOODRUFF (1807–1898), c. 1897. As president, this 1847 pioneer guided the LDS Church toward the twentieth century. Photographers: Fox and Symons. Opposite: PIONEERS OF 1847, July 24, 1897. Photographer: George Edward Anderson. Of the 1897 honoring of the immigrants, pioneer Christopher Jacobs wrote, "Little did we think at the time that our suffering should be remembered at this late day and our work commemorated by an appreciative posterity in a great jubilee. . . . Many of the Old Pioneers have crossed to the other side and those now remaining will soon follow; but their work shall never die."[9]

TRAIL & MORMON CHRONOLOGY

1801   *June 1*—Brigham Young is born in Whitingham, Vermont.

1803   Louisiana Purchase; the United States buys lands between the Mississippi River and the Rocky Mountains from France.

1804   Lewis and Clark lead Corp of Discovery on a 5,000-mile, round-trip exploration of the West, from the Missouri River to the Pacific Ocean.

1805   *December 23*—Joseph Smith is born in Sharon, Vermont.

1807   The first trappers go up the Missouri River in search of beaver.

1810   Fur trappers enter the Southwest.

1812   Trappers returning east from the Columbia River discover Wyoming's South Pass.

1820   *Spring*—Near Palmyra, New York, 14-year-old Joseph Smith reports a vision of God the Father and Jesus Christ.

1821   Trade along the Santa Fe Trail begins.

1824   Mountain man Jedediah Smith's party opens the way west as they rediscover Wyoming's South Pass.

Jim Bridger is the first white man to see the Great Salt Lake.

1825   The first mountain man rendezvous, at Henry's Fork of the Green River.

1827   *September 22*—Joseph Smith receives ancient gold plates from the angel Moroni and begins their translation.

1830   *March*—The Book of Mormon is published at Palmyra, New York.

April 6—The Church of Christ is established

(renamed The Church of Jesus Christ of Latter-day Saints in 1838).

Jedediah Smith leads the first covered wagons from the Missouri River into the Rocky Mountains.

1831 *February*—Joseph Smith arrives in Kirtland, Ohio; the body of the Latter-day Saints soon follow.

Autumn—A group of Mormons settle near Independence (Jackson County), Missouri.

1832 *March 24*—Joseph Smith and his counselor Sidney Rigdon are tarred and feathered at Hiram, Ohio.

June—Brigham Young converts to Mormonism.

1833 *November 7*—Mobs force Mormons to flee Jackson County, Missouri.

1834 *May–June*—Zion's Camp, 200 armed men led by Joseph Smith, sets out from Ohio to help persecuted Mormons 900 miles away in Missouri. The camp fails to stop the persecutions.

Fort William (later Fort Laramie, Wyoming) is built by fur trappers William Sublette and Robert Campbell.

Fort Hall (Idaho) is established by fur trapper N. J. Wyeth.

1836 *March 27*—The Kirtland Temple is dedicated—the first Mormon temple.

Autumn—Missouri Saints are forced to leave Clay County; they settle in Caldwell County.

As part of a Protestant missionary group bound for Oregon, Eliza Spalding and Narcissa Whitman are the first white women to cross the Rocky Mountains.

1837 *June 13*—Missionaries leave Kirtland bound for England to establish the first Mormon foreign mission—the British Mission.

July 30—The first British converts are baptized (nine of them). By year's end another 991 join the LDS Church. From 1846 to 1869 some 32,000 British and Irish converts emigrate to Utah.

1838 *January 12*—Their lives threatened, Joseph Smith and other Church leaders leave Kirtland for Missouri. By midsummer the majority of the Kirtland Saints have set out for Missouri.

March 14—Far West, Missouri, becomes the new Mormon Church headquarters.

April 26—The Church of Christ is renamed The Church of Jesus Christ of Latter-day Saints.

August 6—Election day fist-fight between Mormons and Missourians, Gallatin, Missouri.

October 25—The Battle of Crooked River;

several Mormons are killed, including apostle David Patten.

October 27—Missouri Governor Boggs issues orders to have Mormons exterminated or driven from the state.

October 30—During a truce, a Missouri mob massacres 17 Saints and wounds 13 others at Haun's Mill.

October 31—Joseph Smith and others are arrested by militia.

December 1—Joseph Smith and five other Mormons are imprisoned in Liberty Jail, Missouri.

Cherokee Indians' "Trail of Tears."

1839   *February*—Under Brigham Young's direction, scattered refugee Saints begin arriving at Quincy, Illinois.

April—Joseph Smith and fellow prisoners are allowed to "escape" and make their way to Illinois.

Commerce (renamed Nauvoo), Illinois, is chosen as the next Mormon settlement. It will be the Church's headquarters from 1839 to 1846.

1840   *June 6*—Forty-one English Mormons leave Liverpool for the United States, the first foreign Saints to migrate to America. Some 85,000

foreign-born Mormons emigrate to the United States by the end of the century.

December 16—The Illinois General Assembly passes the Nauvoo Charter, granting Nauvoo city status, a university, and a city militia.

Summer—The last mountain-man rendezvous, near Green River, Wyoming.

1841   *April 6*—Cornerstones are laid for the Nauvoo Temple.

The first large group (the Bidwell-Bartleson party of 48 wagons) migrates over the Oregon Trail to California.

1842   *May*—Missouri Ex-Governor Boggs is wounded by a gunman; Joseph Smith's body guard Orrin P. Rockwell is charged and later acquitted.

May 4—Joseph Smith introduces the endowment, a sacred Mormon temple rite.

August 6—Joseph Smith prophesies that the Saints will be driven into the Rocky Mountains.

Colonel John C. Fremont heads a U.S. expedition to explore the Rocky Mountains.

1843   *July 12*—Joseph Smith records a revelation on "Eternity of Marriage Covenant and Plural Marriage."

Nine hundred Oregon-bound emigrants follow the Oregon Trail.

1844   *January 29*—Joseph Smith begins his candidacy for U.S. president.

February 20—Joseph Smith instructs LDS Church leaders to organize an expedition to explore possible settlement in Oregon or California.

June 7—The anti-Mormon *Nauvoo Expositor* newspaper is published.

June 10—Joseph Smith declares the *Nauvoo Expositor* a nuisance and has the press destroyed.

June 23—Accused of treason, Joseph Smith and his brother Hyrum submit to arrest and are jailed at Carthage, Illinois.

June 27—Joseph and Hyrum Smith are murdered at Carthage Jail, Illinois.

August 8—Brigham Young assumes leadership of the Mormon Church.

1845   *January*—The Illinois legislature revokes the Nauvoo Charter.

May 30—In a rigged trial, accused assassins of the Smiths are acquitted.

September—Responding to increased anti-Mormon violence, Brigham Young announces that Mormons will leave Illinois in the spring. An estimated 3,000 non-LDS emigrants follow the Oregon Trail to Oregon.

The first use of the term *Manifest Destiny,* in *The United States Magazine and Democratic Review.*

1846   *February 4*—Nauvoo Mormons begin crossing the Mississippi River to Iowa; 238 Mormons leave New York for California on the ship *Brooklyn*.

April 24—Westward Saints establish camp at Garden Grove, Iowa.

May 1—The Nauvoo Temple is publicly dedicated.

May 13—The United States declares war on Mexico.

May 18—Mormon encampment at Mt. Pisgah, Iowa.

June 14—Mormon encampment at Council Bluffs.

July 16—The Mormon Battalion is mustered into U.S. service, begins 2,000-mile march.

July 29—The emigrant ship *Brooklyn* arrives in San Francisco.

September 17—The remaining Mormons are driven from Nauvoo after a three-day battle with mobs.

September 23—Winter Quarters (now Florence, Nebraska) is established by the Saints.

The ill-fated Donner Party becomes snow-bound in the Sierra Nevadas.

1847   *April 5*—The vanguard group of the Mormon Pioneer Company leaves Winter Quarters for the Great Basin.

June 28—Brigham Young meets mountain man Jim Bridger. They discuss the trail route into and the feasibility of settling in the Salt Lake Valley.

June 30—Sam Brannan, leader of emigrant ship *Brooklyn,* reports to Brigham Young at the Green River, Wyoming.

July 16—The Mormon Battalion is discharged at Los Angeles.

July 21—Scouts Erastus Snow and Orson Pratt enter the Salt Lake Valley.

July 24—Brigham Young enters the Salt Lake Valley with the first wagon companies.

July 28—Brigham Young selects the site for the Salt Lake Temple.

1848   *January 24*—Gold discovered near Sutter's Mill, California. (Mormon Battalion members present.)

February 2—End of the United States war with Mexico

1849   *Fall*—The Mormon Perpetual Emigration Fund is established to aid poor emigrants.

Kanesville, Iowa, is the "jumping-off" point for Mormon emigrants from 1849 to 1852.

Cholera epidemic along western emigrant trails.

Mass migration of gold-seekers; California's population swells to 100,000.

1850   *September 20*—Brigham Young is appointed governor of the newly established Utah Territory.

Mormons begin missionary efforts in Scandinavia, France, Switzerland, Italy, and Hawaii.

Cholera epidemic along western emigrant trails.

1851   Treaty of Fort Laramie between Plains Indians and U.S. government. The intention is to keep the peace and protect the emigrant trail.

Nationally, the number of emigrants hits a low, one-fifth the number of 1850.

1852   *August 29*—Latter-day Saints publicly announce the practice of plural marriage.

Cholera epidemic along western emigrant trails.

1853   *February 14*—Cornerstones are laid for the Salt Lake Temple.

Keokuk, Iowa, is the "jumping-off" point for Mormon emigrants.

1854   Cholera epidemic along the Santa Fe Trail.

1855   *October 29*—In a general epistle, LDS Church

leaders propose that emigrants cross the plains by handcart.

Sporadic outbreaks of cholera along the western emigrant trails.

1856   *June 9*—The first Mormon handcart company leaves Iowa City, Iowa. Ten groups cross the plains by handcart between 1856 and 1860.

Mid-October—The late-leaving Willie and Martin handcart companies are stranded by blizzards.

October 21—The heroic rescue of the Willie handcart company; 68 of 404 in the company die.

October 28—The Martin company is rescued; 145 of 576 die.

November 9—The Willie company arrives in Salt Lake City.

November 30—The Martin company arrives in Salt Lake City.

Iowa City, Iowa, is the "jumping-off" point for Mormon emigrants from 1856 to 1858.

1857   *May 28*—U.S. President Buchanan sends 2,500 troops to Utah with orders to arrest Brigham Young. Beginning of the "Utah War."

July 24—News of the approaching army reaches Salt Lake City.

September 7–11—Mountain Meadows

Massacre; California-bound emigrants are killed by Indians and a group of Mormon zealots.

September 15—Governor Brigham Young declares martial law and forbids U.S. troops to enter the Salt Lake Valley.

October—Mormon Lot Smith and his men harass U.S. troops by burning wagons and driving off livestock.

November 16—U.S. troops winter near Fort Bridger.

1858   *May*—Northern Utah Mormons evacuate settlements in preparation for war with U.S. troops.

June 11—A peaceful settlement of the Utah War is negotiated.

June 26—Federal troops peacefully pass through Salt Lake City on the way to Cedar Valley, 40 miles to the southwest.

July—Mormons return home.

1859   Florence, Nebraska, is the "jumping-off" point for Mormon emigrants.

1860   *September 24*—The last handcart company arrives in Salt Lake City.

The short-lived Pony Express mail service begins.

1861   *April 23*—A Mormon wagon train leaves Salt

Lake City for Florence, Nebraska, to pick up Mormon emigrants. This is the beginning of the ingenious down-and-back system, which will continue until the end of 1868.

August 16—The first down-and-back company arrives in Salt Lake City.

October 18—The transcontinental telegraph is joined in Salt Lake City.

November 20—Final run of the Pony Express.

The U.S. Civil War begins.

1862   The Homestead Act grants citizens 160 acres of public land. 1,623,692 successful applications.

1864   Wyoming, Nebraska, is the "jumping-off" point for Mormon emigrants until 1866.

1865   Because of Utah's Black Hawk Indian War, no down-and-back wagon trains operate. "Independent" Mormon trains continue throughout the travel season. The United States escalates war against the Sioux and by the end of 1876 effectively completes the conquest of the plains tribes.

The Civil War ends.

1867   The Salt Lake Mormon Tabernacle is completed.

No down-and-back wagon trains operate.

1868   Laramie and, later the same summer, Benton, Wyoming, are the "jumping-off" points for Mormon emigrants.

September 25—End of an era: The final LDS Church emigrant wagon train arrives in Salt Lake City.

1869   *May 10*—The driving of the Golden Spike joins the transcontinental railroad at Promontory, Utah.

June 25—The first Mormon company to travel all the way from the Missouri River via railroad arrives in Utah.

1877   *August 29*—Brigham Young dies at age 76.

ACKNOWLEDGMENTS

ON TOP OF THE LIST of acknowledgments is the deep and profound gratitude we owe to each of our families. Bill: To Sheri, my wife, for researching and acquiring images for both the documentary and this book, as well as for her patience and encouragement to "get this done and go skiing!"; and to Danielle for her help and to Wes for his listening to pioneer stories.

Mike: To Loretta, Cristy, and Laura, whose encouragement no one but I can fully appreciate. Thank you for your patience, love, and endless help.

The authors would like to thank their friends and colleagues Mel Bashore, Christy Best, W. Randall Dixon, Chad Orton, and April Williamsen, with a special thank-you to Ron "Sights and Sounds" Barney for his example as well as his ever-present interest and encouragement. We appreciate and acknowledge the work of Ron and Nancy Anderson, Will Bagley, Dave Bigler, Lyndia and Robert Carter, Bill Hartley, Garn Hatch, George Ivory, Kristen Johnson, Stan Kimball, Norma Ricketts, and Hal Schindler, who, by sharing their vast knowledge of America's historic trails, have contributed to this book; all are members of the Oregon-California Trails Association and/or the Utah Westerners. Jere Krakow and Kay Threlkeld of the National Park Service deserve great thanks for their efforts on behalf of trail history. We also thank Susan Arrington Madsen and Maurine Ward for their contributions to Mormon history.

This work would not have been possible without the help of the following people and institutions: Darlene Dueck of the Anchutz Investment Company, Cristina Segovia of the Corcoran Gallery of Art, Sandra Hilderbrand of the Gilcrease Museum, Historian Dean M. Knudsen and Superintendent Larry D. Reed of Scotts Bluff National Monument, John Carter and Kathyrn Wyatt of the Nebraska State Historical Society, Edith Menna of the International Society of Daughters of Utah Pioneers, Ron Romig of the Re-Organized Church of Jesus Christ of Latter Day Saints, Ron Read of the LDS Museum of Church History and Art, Laura Jolley of the Missouri State Archives, the staff of the

Library of Congress, the staff of the National Archives, the staff of the Library and the Archives of the Historical Department of The Church of Jesus Christ of Latter-day Saints, Alan Barnett of the Utah State Historical Society, and Lorraine Crouse, Walter Jones, and Roy Webb of the University of Utah's Marriot Library Special Collections.

Particular thanks go to Gary Dixon of Bonneville Communications, Lee Groberg of Groberg Communications, and Russ Winegar of Panorama Productions. We would like to recognize the efforts of the following people at Shadow Mountain: Sheri Dew, vice-president of publishing; Anne Sheffield, production manager; Jack Lyon, managing editor; Ron Stucki, art director; Patricia J. Parkinson, senior typographer; Andrea Smith, indexer; and Jennifer Pritchett, editorial assistant.

Special acknowledgements from Mike: Thanks to Dr. Kenneth N. Owens, Director of the Capital Campus Public History Program at California State University, Sacramento, who has helped me in countless ways and who, some years ago, initiated my endless fascination with the American West and its historic trails. A special thanks to my close friend and coauthor, Bill Slaughter, whose understanding of the human drama in the epic story of the Mormon Trail found expression in the pages of this book. Simply put, associating with Bill in this project has been a privilege.

Special acknowledgments from Bill: To Mike Landon for his long hours and willingness to share his vast knowledge and love of Western American trail history. To Jeff Cottle and Richard Holzapfel for their friendship, encouragement, and example.

Suggestions for further readings on the American West, overland trails, and Mormon history

Alexander, Thomas G. *Things in Heaven and Earth: The Life and Times of Wilford Woodruff, a Mormon Prophet.* Salt Lake City: Signature Books, 1991.

Allen, James B., and Glen M. Leonard. *The Story of the Latter-day Saints.* Salt Lake City: Deseret Book, 1976.

Arrington, Leonard J. *Great Basin Kingdom: An Economic History of the Latter-day Saints, 1830–1900.* Cambridge: Harvard University Press, 1958; reprint, Lincoln: University of Nebraska Press, 1966.

————. *Brigham Young: American Moses.* New York: Random House, 1985.

Bagley, Pat, and William W. Slaughter, *Church History Time Line.* Salt Lake City: Deseret Book Co., 1996.

Blackburn, Abner. *Frontiersman: Abner Blackburn's Narrative,* edited by Will Bagley. Salt Lake City: University of Utah Press, 1992.

Bennett, Richard E. *Mormons at the Missouri, 1846–1852.* Norman: University of Oklahoma Press, 1987.

Bigler, David L., ed. *The Gold Discovery Journal of Azariah Smith.* Salt Lake City: University of Utah Press, 1990.

Billington, Ray Allen. *The Far Western Frontier, 1830–1860.* New York: Harper and Row, 1956.

Bullock, Thomas. *The Pioneer Camp of the Saints: The 1846 and 1847 Mormon Trail Journals of Thomas Bullock,* edited by Will Bagley. Spokane, Wash.: The Arthur H. Clark Co., 1997.

Carter, Lyndia McDowell. *One Long Funeral March: Story of the Martin Handcart Company.* Salt Lake City: University of Utah (forthcoming).

De Voto, Bernard. *The Year of Decision: 1846.* Boston: Little, Brown, and Co., 1943.

Ellsworth, S. George, ed. *The Journals of Addison Pratt.* Salt Lake City: University of Utah Press, 1990.

Faragher, John Mack. *Women and Men on the Overland Trail.* New Haven: Yale University Press, 1979.

Green, Ephraim. *A Road From El Dorado: The 1848 Trail Journal of Ephraim Green,* edited by Will Bagley. Salt Lake City: Prairie Dog Press, 1991.

Hafen, LeRoy R., and Ann W. Hafen. *Handcarts to Zion: The Story of a Unique Western Migration, 1856–1860.* Glendale, Calif.: Arthur H. Clark Co., 1960.

Hartley, William G. *My Best for the Kingdom: History and Autobiography of John Lowe Butler, a Mormon Frontiersman.* Salt Lake City: Aspen Books, 1993.

Holliday, J. S. *The World Rushed In, the California Gold Rush Experience: An Eyewitness Account of a Nation Headed West.* New York: Simon and Schuster, 1981.

Holzapfel, Richard Neitzel. *Their Faces Toward Zion: Voices and Images of the Trek West.* Salt Lake City: Bookcraft, 1996.

Jeffrey, Julie Roy. *Frontier Women: The Trans-Mississippi West, 1840–1880.* New York: Hill and Wang, 1979.

Kimball, Stanley B. ed. *W. Clayton's The Latter-day Saints Emigrants' Guide.* Gerald, Missouri: The Patrice Press, 1983.

———. *Historic Sites and Markers along the Mormon and Other Great Western Trails.* Urbana: University of Illinois Press, 1988.

———. *Historic Resource Study: Mormon Pioneer National Historic Trail.* U.S. Department of the Interior, National Park Service, 1991.

Korns, J. Roderic, and Dale L. Morgan. *West from Fort Bridger.* Rev. Will Bagley and Harold Schindler. Logan: Utah State University Press, 1994.

Lass, William E. *From the Missouri to the Great Salt Lake: An Account of Overland Freighting.* Lincoln: Nebraska State Historical Society, 1972.

Limerick, Patricia Nelson. *The Legacy of Conquest: The Unbroken Past of the American West.* New York: W. W. Norton, 1987.

Madsen, Brigham D. *Gold Rush Sojourners in Great Salt Lake City: 1849–1850.* Salt Lake City: University of Utah Press, 1983.

Madsen, Susan Arrington. *I Walked to Zion: True Stories of Young Pioneers on the Mormon Trail.* Salt Lake City: Deseret Book Co., 1994.

Mattes, Merrill J. *The Great Platte River Road: The Covered Wagon Mainline via Fort Kearney to Fort Laramie.* Lincoln: Nebraska State Historical Society, 1969.

———. *Platte River Road Narratives.* Urbana: University of Illinois Press, 1988.

May, Dean L. *Family, Land, and Society in the American West, 1850–1900.* New York: Cambridge University Press, 1994.

Mintz, Lannon W. *The Trail: A Bibliography of the Travellers on the Overland Trail to California, Oregon, Salt Lake City, and Montana during the Years 1841–1864.* Albuquerque: University of New Mexico Press, 1987.

Morgan, Dale L. *The Humboldt: Highroad of the West.* New York: Farrer & Rinehart, 1943; reprint, Lincoln: University of Nebraska, 1985.

———. *The Great Salt Lake.* Indianapolis: Bobbs-Merrill, 1947; reprint, Salt Lake City: University of Utah Press, 1995.

Myers, Sandra L. *Ho for California! Women's Overland Diaries from the Huntington Library.* San Marino: Huntington Library, 1980.

———. *Westering Women and the Frontier Experience, 1800–1915.* Albuquerque: University of New Mexico Press, 1982.

Owens, Kenneth N., ed. *John Sutter and a Wider West.* Lincoln: University of Nebraska Press, 1994.

Prucha, Francis Paul. *Atlas of American Indian Affairs.* Lincoln: University of Nebraska Press, 1990.

Ricketts, Norma. *The Mormon Battalion: U.S. Army of the West, 1846–1848.* Logan, Ut.: Utah State University Press, 1996.

Slaughter, William W. *Life in Zion: An Intimate Look at the Latter-day Saints.* Salt Lake City: Deseret Book Co., 1995.

Stegner, Wallace. *The Gathering of Zion.* New York: McGraw-Hill, 1971; reprint, Lincoln: University of Nebraska Press, 1992.

Stewart, George R. *Ordeal By Hunger.* New York: Houghton Mifflin, 1988.

———. *The California Trail.* New York: McGraw-Hill, 1962; Lincoln: University of Nebraska Press, 1983.

Townley, John M. *The Trail West: A Bibliographic Index to Western Trails, 1841–1869.* Reno: Jamison Station Press, 1988.

Unruh, John. *The Plains Across: The Overland Emigrants and the Trans-Mississippi West, 1840–1860.* Urbana: University of Illinois Press, 1979.

Wheat, Carl I. *Mapping the Transmississippi West.* 5 vols. San Francisco: Institute of Historical Cartography, 1957–1963.

White, Richard. *"It's Your Misfortune and None of My Own": A New History of the American West.* Norman: University of Oklahoma Press, 1991.

NOTES

Note: Quotations have occasionally been edited for clarity.

INTRODUCTION

1. Hannah Barwell Saunders, reminiscence, typescript, 1. Used courtesy of Troy Stover.

2. Ibid., 1–2.

3. As quoted in Janet Roberts Balmforth, "Biography of Robert David Roberts," typescript copy courtesy John Balmforth.

4. Margaret Gay Judd Clawson Reminiscence [1904]–1911, 24, microfilm of typescript, Historical Department, Archives Division, The Church of Jesus Christ of Latter-day Saints, Salt Lake City (hereinafter cited as LDS Church Archives).

5. Lucy Marie Canfield Margetts Journal, Oct. 14, 1862, LDS Church Archives.

6. Samuel M. Smucker, *Life Among the Mormons, or the Religious, Social, and Political History of the Mormons* (New York: Hurst and Co., 1889), 315.

7. Wallace Stegner, *The Gathering of Zion: The Story of the Mormon Trail* (Lincoln: University of Nebraska Press, 1992), 6.

8. Ibid., 1.

9. "The Last Train," *Frontier Guardian*, July 24, 1849.

CHAPTER 1: THE BEGINNING: "WHERE DID THEY COME FROM?"

1. John Benson, Journal, July 24, 1849, photocopy of typescript (original typescript at Nebraska State Historical Society), LDS Church Archives.

2. Joseph Smith, *History of The Church of Jesus Christ of Latter-day Saints,* 2nd ed., rev., edited by B. H. Roberts, 7 vols. (Salt Lake City: The Church of Jesus Christ of Latter-day Saints, 1932–51) 1:5–6.

3. Ibid. 1:11–12.

4. *The Doctrine and Covenants of The Church of Jesus Christ of Latter-day Saints* (Salt Lake City: The Church of Jesus Christ of Latter-day Saints, 1981; hereinafter cited as D&C) 29:8.

5. *History of the Church* 1:261–64.

6. D&C 57:2–3.

7. Lilburn Boggs, Extermination Order, Oct. 27, 1838, holograph, Missouri State Archives.

8. *History of the Church* 3:190–91, note.

9. Ibid. 3:375.

10. As quoted in B. H. Roberts, *A Comprehensive History of The Church of Jesus Christ of Latter-day Saints, Century One,* 6 vols. (Salt Lake City: The Church of Jesus Christ of Latter-day Saints, 1930) 2:190.

11. As quoted in Carol Cornwall Madsen, *In Their Own Words: Women and the Story of Nauvoo* (Salt Lake City: Deseret Book Co., 1994), 180.

12. Luman Andros Shurtliff Journal, May 1841–Apr. 1856, microfilm of holograph, LDS Church Archives, 242.

13. *Nauvoo Neighbor,* October 29, 1845.

14. In Edward W. Tullidge, *The Women of Mormondom* (New York: Tullidge & Crandall, 1877), 342–43.

CHAPTER 2: THE IOWA TREK: "A CONTINUOUS MUD HOLE"

1. "Diary of Lorenzo Dow Young," *Utah Historical Quarterly* 14 (1946): 133.

2. Manuscript history of Brigham Young as quoted in Roberts, *A Comprehensive History* 3:45–46.

3. *Hancock Eagle* as reprinted in the *Illinois Gazette,* May 9, 1846.

4. William Byram Pace, Autobiography [c. 1904], microfilm of ms., LDS Church Archives.

5. Abner Blackburn, *Frontiersman: Abner Blackburn's Narrative,* edited by Will Bagley (Salt Lake City: University of Utah Press, 1992), 26.

6. Helen Mar Kimball Whitney, Autobiography, typescript, Harold B. Lee Library, Special Collections, Brigham Young University.

7. William Clayton, *William Clayton's Journal* (Salt Lake City: Clayton Family Organization, 1921), 3–7.

8. Erastus Snow, Journals, 1835–1857, vol. 3, LDS Church Archives.

9. Wayne Stout, *Hosea Stout: Utah's Pioneer Statesman* (Salt Lake City: Wayne Stout, 1953), 66–67; Stanley B. Kimball, *Historic Resource Study: Mormon Pioneer National Historic Trail* (United States Department of the Interior, National Park Service, 1991), 77; Russell R. Rich, *Ensign to the Nations* (Provo, Ut.: Brigham Young University Publications, 1972), 13.

10. "Extracts from Eliza R. Snow's Private Journal," LDS Church Archives.

11. For additional information on the trail variants at Drakesville see Stanley B. Kimball, "The Mormon Trail Network in Iowa 1838–1863: A New Look," *BYU Studies* 21 (Fall 1981): 419.

12. Snow, Journals, 1835–1857, vol. 3.

13. Orson Pratt, *The Orson Pratt Journals,* compiled by Elden J. Watson (Salt Lake City, 1975), 329

14. Frederick Piercy, *Route from Liverpool to Great Salt Lake Valley,* edited by James Linforth (Liverpool: Franklin D. Richards, 1855), 85.

15. Blackburn, *Frontiersman,* 26.

16. Emily Smith Hoyt, Reminiscences and diary, 1851–1893, microfilm, LDS Church Archives.

17. As quoted in Susan Arrington Madsen, *I Walked to Zion: True Stories of Young Pioneers on the Mormon Trail* (Salt Lake City: Deseret Book Co., 1994), 37.

18. Clawson, Reminiscence.

19. John D. Lee, Journal, Feb. 17, 1846, LDS Church Archives.

20. Sarah Rich, Autobiography, typescript, Harold B. Lee Library, Special Collections, Brigham Young University, in Milton V. Backman and Keith Perkins, *Writings of Early Latter-day Saints and Their Contemporaries* (Provo, Ut., 1989).

21. *Hancock Eagle* as reprinted in the *Illinois Gazette,* May 6, 1846.

22. Zina Huntington Young as quoted in Tullidge, *The Women of Mormondom,* 328.

23. Rich, Autobiography.

24. Clayton, *William Clayton's Journal,* 19.

25. Brigham Young to A. W. Babbitt, John L. Heywood, and J. S. Fullmer, Nauvoo Trustees, Apr. 12, 1846, Brigham Young Papers, LDS Church Archives.

26. Parley P. Pratt, *Autobiography of Parley P. Pratt,* edited by Parley P. Pratt, Jr. (Salt Lake City: Deseret Book, 1961), 342.

27. Zerah Pulsipher, Autobiography, Harold B. Lee Library, Special Collections, Brigham Young University.

28. Allen Joseph Stout, Reminiscences and journal, 1845–1889, LDS Church Archives.

29. Pratt, *Autobiography,* 342.

30. *Sangamo Journal* (Springfield, Ill.), July 23, 1846.

31. Benjamin Chamberlain Critchlow, Autobiography, carbon copy of typescript, LDS Church Archives, 3.

32. Louisa Barnes Pratt, Autobiography, in Kate B. Carter, ed., *Heart Throbs of the West* (Salt Lake City: Daughters of the Utah Pioneers), 8:239.

33. Philemon Merrill, typescript of autobiography, LDS Church Archives.

34. John Pulsipher, *A Short Sketch of the History of John Pulsipher, the Son of Zerah Pulsipher* (1970), 10.

35. Thomas Bullock to Willard Richards, Sept. 1846, Brigham Young Collection, LDS Church Archives.

36. Thomas L. Kane's lecture *The Mormons* as quoted in Roberts, *A Comprehensive History* 3:135; Daniel Tyler, *A Concise History of the Mormon Battalion in the Mexican War, 1846–1847* (repr.), (Chicago: Rio Grande Press, 1964), 64–106.

37. Journal History, May 3, 1846, as quoted in Richard Bennett, *Mormons at the Missouri, 1846–1852* (Norman: University of Oklahoma Press, 1987), 42.

38. Luman Shurtliff, Autobiography, typescript at the Harold B. Lee Library, Special Collections, Brigham Young University, in Backman and Perkins, *Writings of Early Latter-day Saints.*

39. Thomas Bullock, Journal, Oct. 9, 1846, LDS Church Archives.

40. John H. Krenkel, ed., *The Life and Times of Joseph Fish, Mormon Pioneer* (Danville, Ill.: The Interstate Printers & Publishers, Inc.), 21.

41. Henry William Bigler, Journal, Feb. 1846–Oct. 1899, microfilm of ms., LDS Church Archives.

42. Manuscript History of Brigham Young as quoted in Roberts, *A Comprehensive History* 3:81.

43. James S. Brown, *Life of a Pioneer* (Salt Lake City: Geo. Q. Cannon & Sons, 1900), 23.

44. Ibid.

45. Zadoc Judd, Autobiography, typescript of ms., LDS Church Archives, 21.

46. Norton Jacob, *The Record of Norton Jacob,* edited by C. Edward Jacob and Ruth Jacob (Salt Lake City: The Norton Jacob Family Association, 1949), 29.

47. Lucy Meserve Smith, Autobiography, 1888–1890, typescript, LDS Church Archives.

48. Margaret Phelps as quoted in Bennett, *Mormons at the Missouri, 1846–1852,* 79–80.

49. Merrill J. Mattes, *The Great Platte River Road: The Covered Wagon Mainline via Fort Kearny to Fort Laramie* (Lincoln: University of Nebraska Press, 1987), 90.

50. Blackburn, *Frontiersman,* 26.

51. "Report of Daniel D. McArthur," Journal History, September 26, 1856, LDS Church Archives, 5.

CHAPTER 3: FLEEING TO ZION: THE MORMON TRAIL TO THE VALLEY OF THE GREAT SALT LAKE

1. Jacob, *The Record of Norton Jacob,* 29.

2. Ibid., 32.

3. Brigham Young to Joseph A. Stratton, Feb. 18, 1847, as quoted in Carl I. Wheat, *Mapping the Transmississippi West* (San Francisco: Institute of Historical Cartography, 1959) 3:31.

4. Jacob, *The Record of Norton Jacob,* 33.

5. Sylvester Henry Earl, Autobiographical Sketch, 1854, typescript of ms., LDS Church Archives, 5.

6. "History of George Albert Smith [c. 1834–1871]," typescript, LDS Church Archives.

7. Appleton Milo Harmon, Journal, Apr. 21, 1847, LDS Church Archives.

8. Levi Jackman, Journal, Apr. 21, 1847, photocopy of ms., LDS Church Archives.

9. William M. Egan, ed., *Pioneering the West, 1846 to 1878: Major Howard Egan's Diary* (Richmond, Ut.: Howard R. Egan Estate, 1917), 27.

10. Ibid., 30.

11. Bullock, Journal, Apr. 25, 1847.

12. Egan, *Pioneering the West,* 33.

13. For examples of the Mormon use of the Platte's north side see the *Millennial Star,* Sept. 1, 1849; Thomas Steed, *The Life of Thomas Steed from His Own Diary, 1826–1910* (Farmington, Ut., 1935), 15.

14. Harmon, Journal, May 7, 1847.

15. Clayton, *William Clayton's Journal,* 143–44, 151–52.

16. Harmon, Journal, May 20, 1847.

17. Ibid., May 20–22, 1847.

18. John Brown, *Autobiography of Pioneer John Brown, 1820–1896,* edited by John Zimmerman Brown (Salt Lake City: Stevens & Wallis, Inc., 1941), 74.

19. Egan, *Pioneering the West,* 43.

20. Ibid., 54–57.

21. Clayton, *William Clayton's Journal,* 201.

22. John Steele as quoted in Blackburn, *Frontiersman,* 61, note 40.

23. Ibid., 61.

24. Lyman to Young, June 28, 1847, Brigham Young Collection, LDS Church Archives.

25. Brown, *Autobiography,* 75.

26. James Godson Bleak, Journal, 1853–1860, LDS Church Archives.

27. Levi Hammon Emigrating Company, Journal, June–Sept. 1851, microfilm of ms., LDS Church Archives; Almira Tiffany Bethers, "Biography of Mary Jane Bethers York," typescript, LDS Church Archives.

28. James Henry Rollins, Reminiscences 1896; 1898; typescript of ms., LDS Church Archives.

29. Diana Eldredge Smoot, Autobiography, Harold B. Lee Library, Special Collections.

30. The Miner G. Atwood Company was composed mostly of Danish emigrants on their way to the Salt Lake Valley. Seven were injured in the skirmish, and one woman was kidnapped. Miner G. Atwood, Journal, as quoted in the Journal History, Nov. 8, 1865, 8–22.

31. For an account of Indian emigrant relations on the trail in the 1860s, see Brigham Dwaine Madsen, *The Shoshoni Frontier and the Bear River Massacre* (Salt Lake City: University of Utah Press, 1985) and Unruh, *The Plains Across.*

32. Isabella M. Horne, "Pioneer Reminiscences," *Young Women's Journal* 13 (July 1902): 7, 292–93.

33. Kate B. Carter, ed., *Our Pioneer Heritage* (Salt Lake City: Daughters of Utah Pioneers, 1970) 13:463–65.

34. Maybelle Harmon Anderson, ed., *Appleton Milo Harmon Goes West* (Berkeley: Gillick Press, 1946), 173–74.

35. John Pulsipher, *The Journal of John Pulsipher* (1970), 20–30.

36. Reminiscences of Christopher Jacobs in "Biographies and History of Garfield County Pioneers," Daughters of Utah Pioneers, Garfield County Chapter, book A, 114–15.

37. George Benjamin Wallace Emigrating Company, Journal, LDS Church Archives.

38. Hezekiah Mitchell, Journal, June–Sept. 1854, typescript of ms., LDS Church Archives.

39. John Parry, Reminiscences and diary, Mar. 1857–Sept. 1867, photocopy of ms., LDS Church Archives.

40. Jacob, *The Record of Norton Jacob,* 55.

41. Wilford Woodruff, *Wilford Woodruff's Journal, 1833–1898,* edited by Scott G. Kenney (Midvale, Ut.: Signature Books, 1983) 3:192–93.

42. Ibid., 193.

43. Harmon, Journal, June 2, 1847.

44. Jacob, *The Record of Norton Jacob,* 56.

45. Woodruff, *Wilford Woodruff's Journal* 3:205–6.

46. Ibid., 219–20.

47. Ibid., 220.

48. Ibid.

49. John Steele as quoted in Blackburn, *Frontiersman,* 55.

50. Horace Kimball Whitney as quoted in ibid., 53.

51. William Clayton as quoted in J. Roderic Korns and Dale L. Morgan, eds., *West from Fort Bridger* (Logan, Ut.: Utah State University Press, 1994), 132, 209.

52. Clayton, *William Clayton's Journal,* 291.

53. Albert Perry Rockwood, Diary, Apr.–July 1847, LDS Church Archives.

54. Clayton, *William Clayton's Journal,* 296.

55. Blackburn, *Frontiersman,* 61.

56. Orson Pratt, Journal, July 21, 1847, LDS Church Archives.

57. Jacob, *The Record of Norton Jacob*, 70.

58. Blackburn, *Frontiersman*, 62; Bullock, Journal, July 1847.

59. Identifying their experience as similar to that of the children of Israel also played a role in shaping the later Mormon view of the Salt Lake Valley as a desert. For an overview of the Salt Lake Valley environment at the time the Mormons arrived and Mormon-perceived biblical parallels, see Richard H. Jackson, "The Mormon Experience: the plains as Sinai, the Great Salt Lake as the Dead Sea, and the Great Basin as desert-cum-promised land," *Journal of Historical Geography* 18 (Jan. 1992).

60. Harriett Young entry in Lorenzo Dow Young, Journals, 1846–1852, LDS Church Archives.

61. Woodruff, *Wilford Woodruff's Journal* 3:233.

62. "Manuscript History of Brigham Young" as quoted in Roberts, *A Comprehensive History* 3:223–24.

63. Patty Bartlett Sessions, Diaries and Account Book, 1846–1866, 1880, typescript of ms., LDS Church Archives, 47–48.

64. Bullock, Journal, Sept. 5, 1847.

65. Hyde, *The Private Journal of William Hyde*, 46.

66. Ibid., 47–48.

67. Ibid., 48–49.

68. William Clayton journal as quoted in *An Intimate Chronicle: The Journals of William Clayton*, edited by George D. Smith (Salt Lake City: Signature Books, 1991), 300.

69. George Teasdale, Sixtus E. Johnson Emigrating Company Journal, August 16, 1861, microfilm of typescript, LDS Church Archives.

70. Clawson, Reminiscence.

71. James Henry Linford, Sr., *An Autobiography of James Henry Linford, Sr.* (John Linford Family Organization, 1947), 25.

CHAPTER 4: THE GOLD RUSH AND THE END OF ISOLATION

1. Richard Ballantyne, Journal, June 25, 1848, LDS Church Archives.

2. Oliver Boardman Huntington, Diary and reminiscences, June 1843–Jan. 1900, LDS Church Archives.

3. Jacob Gates would faithfully serve two missions to Europe, lead emigrants to the Salt Lake Valley in 1853 as a captain, become a member of the Church's First Council of Seventy, serve as a colonel in Utah's Nauvoo Legion militia, and be elected as a legislator from Kane and Washington counties in southern Utah. Andrew Jenson, an assistant Church Historian, wrote, "After a well spent life Elder Gates died at his residence in Provo, Utah county, Utah, April 14, 1892, as a true and faithful Latter-day Saint." Andrew Jenson, *Latter-day Saint Biographical Encyclopedia* (Salt Lake City: Andrew Jenson History Company, 1901) 1:197–98.

4. James S. Brown, *Life of a Pioneer* (Salt Lake City: Geo. Q. Cannon & Sons, 1900), 15.

5. While both Melissa and William made it to the Salt Lake Valley, William's health, already poor, continued to deteriorate. Within a year Melissa was a widow. She then married as a polygamous wife William Henry Kimball, eldest son of Apostle Heber C. Kimball, and successfully managed their stage station at Kimball Junction near present-day Park City, Utah. For an excellent account of Melissa's life in the Mormon Battalion see Norma B. Ricketts, *Melissa's Journey with the Mormon Battalion: The Western Odyssey of Melissa Burton Coray, 1846–1848* (Salt Lake City: International Society, Daughters of the Utah Pioneers, 1994).

6. Brown, *Life of a Pioneer*, 15.

7. Henry W. Bigler as quoted in J. Roderic Korns and Dale L. Morgan, eds., *West from Fort Bridger: The Pioneering of the Immigrant Trails Across Utah, 1846–1850*, rev., Will Bagley and Harold Schindler (Logan: Utah State University Press, 1994), 283.

8. What little is known of Hensley's difficulties on the Salt Desert comes from an account left by Richard Martin May, who was traveling in the James Clyman westbound wagon train that was overtaken by Hensley and his packers on Goose Creek on August 17. There is also a brief account in the Journal History. See Korns and Morgan, *West from Fort Bridger*, 277–306 and Journal History, August 9, 1848.

9. Melissa Coray to Sarah Austin, October 1849, as quoted in Norma Ricketts, *Melissa's Journey with the Mormon Battalion* (Salt Lake City: International Society, Daughters of the Utah Pioneers, 1994), 104.

10. The idea of colonizing hard-to-reach marginal land continued as an LDS policy for decades. George Q. Cannon, commenting on the Arizona colonization effort of the 1870s, stated, "If there be deserts in Arizona, thank God for the deserts. . . . If we find a little oasis in the desert where a few can settle, thank God for the oasis, and thank him for the almost interminable road that lies between that oasis and so-called civilization. . . . The worst places in the land we can probably get, and we must develop them. If we were to find a good country how long would it be before the wicked would want it and strip us of our possessions?" (*Journal of Discourses*, 26 vols. [London: Latter-day Saints' Book Depot, 1854–86] 16:143.)

11. A. G. Lawrence, May 15, 1849, Forth Leavenworth, to the *Cleveland Herald* as reprinted in the *Millennial Star* 11 (Aug. 1, 1849): 239.

12. As reprinted in *Millennial Star* 11 (Sept. 1, 1849): 268.

13. Randolph B. Marcy, *The Prairie Traveler*, reprint (New York: Perigee Books, 1994), 54.

14. Woodruff, *Journal*, 563–65.

15. John Powell Autobiography and journal, Aug. 1, 1856, microfilm of typescript, LDS Church Archives.

16. George A. Smith and William I. Appleby to Orson Pratt as printed in the Journal History, August 12, 1849.

17. Clawson, Reminiscences, 28–29.

18. William I. Appleby, Journal, October 7, 1849, as printed in the Journal History, October 29, 1849.

19. In Dale L. Morgan, "Mormon Ferry on the North Platte," *Annals of Wyoming* 21 (July–Oct. 1949): 113.

20. Ibid., 114.

21. In Dale L. Morgan, "The Ferries of the Forty-Niners," *Annals of Wyoming* (April 1959), 23.

22. Peter Hansen, Journal, as printed in the Journal History, Aug. 7, 1849.

23. As quoted in Morgan, "The Ferries of the Forty-Niners," 63.

24. Brigham D. Madsen, *Gold Rush Sojourners in Great Salt Lake City 1849 and 1850* (Salt Lake City: University of Utah Press, 1983), 33, 114–16; see also Leonard J. Arrington, *Great Basin Kingdom: Economic History of the Latter-day Saints, 1830–1900* (Cambridge: Harvard University Press, 1958; repr. Lincoln: University of Nebraska Press, 1966), 68, 441n.

25. Vincent A. Hoover, Journal, Aug. 15, 1849, microfilm of typescript in the Dale Morgan Papers, Special Collections, Marriott Library, University of Utah.

26. Ben Carpenter to Charles Carpenter, July 17, 1849, LDS Church Archives.

27. William Scearce to David or Jonathan Scearce, July 14, 1849, LDS Church Archives.

28. Arthur Shearer, Journal, Oct. 1, 1849, microfilm of typescript in the Dale Morgan Papers, Special Collections, Marriott Library, University of Utah.

29. George W. Withers to Mr. Miller, Editor of the [Liberty] Tribune, Aug. 12, 1849, microfilm of typescript in the Dale Morgan Papers, Special Collections, Marriott Library, University of Utah.

30. Samuel Kendall Gifford, Reminiscences, 1864, typescript, LDS Church Archives, 7–8.

31. Steed, *The Life of Thomas Steed,* 15.

32. Reminiscences of George Bryant Gardner in James Albert Jones, comp., *Some Early Pioneers of Huntington, Utah, and Surrounding Area* (1980), 90.

33. Krenkel, *The Life and Times of Joseph Fish,* 30.

34. Ibid., 26.

35. Gifford, Reminiscences, 28.

36. Krenkel, *The Life and Times of Joseph Fish,* 25–29

37. John D. Lee as quoted in Eugene E. Campbell, *Establishing Zion: The Mormon Church in the American West, 1847–1859* (Salt Lake City: Signature Books, 1988), 54.

38. Ibid, 54–55.

39. William Butler [Autobiography] as quoted in *An Enduring Legacy* (Salt Lake City: Daughters of the Utah Pioneers, 1985) 8:77.

40. Nelson Wheeler Whipple, Autobiography and journal, August 1850, LDS Church Archives.

41. Isaac Julian Harvey, "Recollections of a Journey to California in 1850," Bancroft Library, University of California, Berkeley.

42. Address of George A. Smith July 24, 1852, *Journal of Discourses* 1:45.

43. John D. Lee as quoted in Campbell, *Establishing Zion,* 54.

44. George Mayer, Reminiscences and Diary, Jan. 1853–Apr. 1896, LDS Church Archives.

45. Joseph Holbrook as quoted in Arrington, *Great Basin Kingdom,* 71.

46. "Incidents in the Life of George Washington Hill written in Ogden City January 2, 1878," Microfilm of ms., Special Collections, Harold B. Lee Library, Brigham Young University.

47. See Leslie T. Foy, *The City Bountiful* (Bountiful, Ut.: Horizon Publishers, 1975), 71–73.

48. The upward pressure on prices increased as emigrants traveled west. At Fort Laramie flour sold for $11.00 per hundred pounds, but by the time the California-bound emigrant reached Ragtown or the Carson Valley trading posts, flour prices were often $2.50 *per pound* or a staggering $250.00 per hundred pounds. See John D. Unruh, Jr., *The Plains Across: The Overland Emigrants and the Trans-Mississippi West, 1840–1860* (Urbana: University of Illinois Press, 1979), 276; and Foy, *The City Bountiful,* 72.

49. First Presidency circular as quoted in Campbell, *Establishing Zion,* 53.

50. Barry, "Overland to the Gold Fields of California in 1852," 271.

51. Hubert Howe Bancroft, *History of Utah, 1540–1886* (San Francisco: The History Company, 1889), 309.

52. Jackman, Journal, April 23, 1847, photocopy of ms., LDS Church Archives.

53. Blackburn, *Frontiersman,* 62.

54. Jonathan Ellis Layne as quoted in the Journal History, Sept. 27, 1852, LDS Church Archives.

55. Smith, Autobiography, typscript of ms., LDS Church Archives, 11.

56. Ballantyne, Journal, June 24, 1848, LDS Church Archives.

57. Pulsipher, Journal, 1970, LDS Church Archives, 22.

58. Carter, *Heart Throbs of the West* 11:162.

59. Sessions, Journal, typescript of ms., LDS Church Archives.

60. Journal of Thomas Bullock as quoted in the Journal History, June 4, 1848, LDS Church Archives.

61. Jacob, *The Record of Norton Jacob,* 33.

62. Arthur Donald Coleman, *Pratt Pioneers of Utah* (Provo, Ut.: J. Grant Stevenson, 1967), 28.

CHAPTER 5: GATHERING TO ZION: THE EMERGING CHURCH EMIGRATION SYSTEM AND THE MORMON TRAIL

1. The First Presidency to Orson Hyde, Oct. 16, 1849, *Millennial Star* 12 (April 1, 1850): 125 as quoted in Arrington, *Great Basin Kingdom,* 78–79.

2. The First Presidency to Orson Hyde, Oct. 16, 1849, *Millennial Star* 12 (April 1, 1850): 124–25 as quoted in Gustive O. Larson, *Prelude to the Kingdom: Mormon Desert Conquest, a Chapter in American Cooperative Experience* (Francestown, N.H.: Marshall Jones Co., 1947), 107–9.

3. *Millennial Star* 14 (January 15, 1852): 23.

4. Ibid., 29.

5. James A. Little, *From Kirtland to Salt Lake City* (Salt Lake City, 1890), 230 as quoted in Larson, *Prelude to the Kingdom,* 112.

6. *Millennial Star* 14 (July 17, 1852): 325.

7. Christian Nielsen, Diary, Feb. 1853–Apr. 1858, typescript of ms. translated from Danish to English, LDS Church Archives, 12–13, 20–22, 33–35.

8. Brigham Young to Franklin D. Richards, April 2, 1854, in Church Immigration Book, 1850–1854, LDS Church Archives.

9. Brigham Young to Franklin D. Richards, Sept. 30, 1855, *Millennial Star* 17 (December 22, 1855): 814–15 as quoted in Larson, *Prelude to the Kingdom,* 100.

10. Hindley, Journals.

11. Heber C. Kimball to Franklin D. Richards, Aug. 31, 1855, reprinted in Journal History, Aug. 31, 1855, 3.

12. Feramorz Y. Fox, "The Mormon Land System: A Study of the Settlement and Utilization of Land Under the Direction of the Mormon Church" (Ph.D. diss., Northwestern University, 1932), 78.

13. Wilford Woodruff to Dr. Asa Fitch, July 31, 1856, reprinted in Journal History, July 31, 1856, 2.

14. William Chandless, *Visit to Salt Lake,* as quoted in Fox, "The Mormon Land System," 81.

15. Brigham Young to Franklin D. Richards, Sept. 30, 1855, reprinted in Journal History, Oct. 29, 1855, 2.

16. Stegner, *The Gathering of Zion,* 221.

17. George Cunningham, Reminiscences, 1876, typescript, LDS Church Archives.

18. LeRoy H. Hafen and Ann W. Hafen, *Handcarts to Zion* (Glendale, Calif.: The Arthur H. Clark Company, 1960), 96–97.

19. John Chislett as quoted in ibid., 99.

20. Ibid., 101.

21. Brigham Young's address reported in the *Deseret News,* Oct. 15, 1856, as quoted in Hafen and Hafen, *Handcarts to Zion,* 120–21.

22. John Chislett as quoted in ibid., 104–6.

23. Mary Hurren Wight, Reminiscences, 1936, in "James G. Willie History," LDS Church Archives, 12.

24. Ibid.

25. *Deseret News,* Nov. 19, 1856, as quoted in Hafen and Hafen, *Handcarts to Zion,* 116–17.

26. Josiah Rogerson, *Salt Lake Tribune,* Jan. 14, 1914, 293, as quoted in Hafen and Hafen, *Handcarts to Zion,* 109.

27. Elizabeth Jackson as quoted in ibid., 109–12.

28. Josiah Rogerson, Reminiscences, in "Handcart Stories," LDS Church Archives, 19–20.

29. William Lawrence Spicer Binder, Reminiscences, LDS Church Archives.

30. Sketches of the life of Mary Lawson Kirkman, Pioneer Histories Camp Springville (Springville, Ut.: Daughters of the Utah Pioneers, 1936) 1:2.

31. John Chislett as quoted in Hafen and Hafen, *Handcarts to Zion,* 130.

32. Stegner, *The Gathering of Zion,* 259.

33. Ibid., 256.

34. Hafen and Hafen, *Handcarts to Zion,* 111–12.

35. James Godson Bleak, Journal, Nov. 30, 1856, LDS Church Archives.

36. Ibid., Sept. 15, 1856–Apr. 9, 1857.

CHAPTER 6: DOWN-AND-BACK YEARS: "OUR MOUNTAIN BOYS WENT ALONG FULL OF BOLDNESS"

1. "Arrivals from the Plains," *Deseret News,* October 10, 1860.

2. Ibid.

3. Ibid.

4. History of the Church 1839–[c. 1882], Apr. 1861, 172–73, Historian's Office, LDS Church Archives.

5. Ibid., Feb. 28, 1861, 93–94.

6. See Arrington, *Great Basin Kingdom,* 208; Roberts, *A Comprehensive History* 5:109–11; Andrew Jenson, *Church Chronology: A Record of Important Events* (Salt Lake City: Deseret News, 1914), 65–78; Church Emigration Books, 1855–1861, 1862–1888, Historian's Office, LDS Church Archives.

7. Joseph M. Tanner, *A Biographical Sketch of John Riggs Murdock* (Salt Lake City: Deseret News, 1909), 152.

8. Ibid., 140.

9. F. W. Blake Diary, July 7 and Aug. 21, 1861, microfilm of holograph, LDS Church Archives.

10. George Teasdale, Sixtus E. Johnson Emigrating Company Journal, Aug. 23, 1861, microfilm of photocopy of typescript, LDS Church Archives.

11. Mary Jane Mount Tanner, *A Fragment: The Autobiography of Mary Jane Mount Tanner,* edited by Margery W. Ward (Salt Lake City: Tanner Trust Fund, University of Utah Library, 1980), 45.

12. Clawson, Reminiscence, 24.

13. Ibid., 30–31.

14. History of the Church, Feb. 28, 1861, 97–98.

15. Tanner, *Biographical Sketch of John Riggs Murdock,* 136–37.

16. History of the Church, May 11, 1861, 183.

17. Frederick Weight, A short history of the life of Frederick Weight by himself [c. 1895], typescript, LDS Church Archives, 4.

18. William Wood Autobiography [1915], carbon copy of typescript, LDS Church Archives, 21.

19. As quoted in William Mulder and A. Russell Mortensen, eds., *Among the Mormons* (Lincoln: University of Nebraska Press, 1973), 335–36.

20. Linford, *An Autobiography, of James Henry Linford, Sr.,* 22.

21. Church Emigration, 1862–1888, LDS Church Archives.

22. William Wood, Autobiography, 22–23.

23. Linford, *An Autobiography,* 22.

24. Ibid., 23–24.

25. Ibid., 22.

26. Tanner, *Biographical Sketch of John Riggs Murdock,* 139–40.

27. Linford, *An Autobiography,* 24–25.

28. Orley Dewight Bliss, remininscences and diary, July 10, 1864, photocopy of holograph, LDS Church Archives.

29. Peter Anthon Nielsen, reminiscence, 6–8, carbon copy of typescript, LDS Church Archives.

30. Zebulon William Jacobs, Reminiscence and diaries, July 18 and Aug. 6, 1861, microfilm of holograph, LDS Church Archives.

31. Linford, *An Autobiography,* 24.

32. Bliss, diary, July 9 and 19, 1864, LDS Church Archives.

33. Zebulon William Jacobs, diaries, 1861–1877, Aug. 17 and 24, 1861, LDS Church Archives.

34. George Teasdale, Sept. 27, 1861.

35. As quoted in Susan Arrington Madsen, *I Walked to Zion,* 23–24.

36. Ibid., 24.

37. Orley Dewight Bliss, diary, Oct. 8, 1864.

38. See Arrington, *Great Basin Kingdom,* 205–9.

39. Sixtus Ellis Johnson, [Autobiography], *A Voice From the Mountains: Life and Works of Joel Hills Johnson* (Mesa, Az.: Joel Hills Johnson Arizona Committee, 1982), 247.

40. Fredrick Weight, "A Short History of the life of Fredrick Weight by himself," c. 1895, microfilm of typescript, LDS Church Archives.

41. Rachel Emma Woolley Simmons, "Journal of Rachel Emma Woolley Simmons," in Carter, *Heart Throbs of the West* 11:162.

42. Cleo H. Evans, comp., *Curtis Edwin Bolton: Pioneer, Missionary* (Fairfax, Va.: Cleo Evans, 1968), 21.

43. Samuel Harrison Bailey Smith, Reminiscences and diary, microfilm of holograph, LDS Church Archives, [5].

44. Woodruff, Journal, July 8, 1847, microfilm of holograph, LDS Church Archives.

45. Aroet Lucius Hale, *Diary of Aroet Lucious Hale* (194_), 17.

46. Lydia Ann Lake Nelson, "Autobiography," *Pioneer Women of Arizona,* compiled by Roberta Flake Clayton (Mesa, Az., 1969), 432.

47. Blackburn, *Frontiersman,* 60–61.

CHAPTER 7: THE END OF THE TRAIL: AN EPILOGUE

1. *Completion of the Pacific Railroad celebration to-day* [broadside] (Salt Lake City: Telegraph Print, 1869).

2. Union Pacific Railroad poster, May 10, 1869.

3. In Journal History, June 25, 1869, 1.

4. *Collected Discourses,* edited and compiled by Brian H. Stuy (Burbank, Calif.: B.H.S. Publishing, 1991), 4:366.

5. *Messages of the First Presidency of The Church of Jesus Christ of Latter-day Saints, 1833–1964,* compiled by James R. Clark, 6 vols. (Salt Lake City: Bookcraft, 1965–1975), 4:222.

6. *Collected Discourses* 5:188.

7. Brigham Young, *Discourses of Brigham Young,* edited by John A. Widstoe (Salt Lake City: Deseret Book Co., 1925), 734–35.

8. Smith, Autobiographical sketch, typescript, LDS Church Archives, 12.

CREDITS

for Photographs and Illustrations

ENDSHEETS
Westward the Course of Empire Takes Its Way, Emanuel Leutze: Architect of the Capitol, Washington, D.C.

CONTENTS
Mormon emigrants near Coalville: LDS Church Archives.

INTRODUCTION
The Overland Trail. The Anschutz Collection.
Mary Elizabeth and Emma Chase: LDS Church Archives.
Mormon emigrant camp at Wyoming, Nebraska, 1866: LDS Church Archives.
Unidentified pioneer couple: LDS Church Archives.
Wagons en route west: National Archives.

CHAPTER 1
Joseph Smith: Library-Archives, Reorganized Church of Jesus Christ of Latter Day Saints.
Sidney Rigdon: LDS Church Archives.
Lucy Mack Smith: LDS Church Archives.
Kirtland Temple: LDS Church Archives.
"Extermination Order": Missouri State Archives.
Lilburn Boggs: LDS Church Archives.
Haun's Mill: Museum of Art, Brigham Young University.
General Alexander Doniphan: LDS Church Archives.
Liberty Jail: LDS Church Archives.
View of Nauvoo: Museum of Church History and Art, Church of Jesus Christ of Latter-day Saints.
Nauvoo Temple: LDS Church Archives.
Emma Smith and her son David Hyrum Smith: Utah State Historical Society.

Hyrum Smith: LDS Church Archives.
Brigham Young: LDS Church Archives.
Artifacts in this chapter and others: Museum of Church History and Art.

CHAPTER 2
Lorenzo Young: LDS Church Archives.
William Pace: LDS Church Archives.
Abner Blackburn: University of Utah, Special Collections.
Sugar Creek: Museum of Church History and Art.
William Pitt: LDS Church Archives.
Eliza R. Snow: Utah State Historical Society.
Yoking a Wild Bull: Scotts Bluff National Monument.
Mormon pioneers fleeing Nauvoo: D. Appleton and Company.
Drawings from Heber C. Kimball's 1846 diary: LDS Church Archives.
Zina D. H. Young with Willard and Phoebe Young: LDS Church Archives.
William Clayton and Maria Louisa Lyman Clayton: LDS Church Archives.
Parley P. Pratt: LDS Church Archives.
Drawings from Heber C. Kimball's 1846 diary: LDS Church Archives.
Zera and Mary Brown Pulsipher: LDS Church Archives.
Battle of Nauvoo: Museum of Art, Brigham Young University.
Thomas Bullock: LDS Church Archives.
Brigham Young: LDS Church Archives.
Catching Quail: Museum of Art, Brigham Young University.
Zadoc Judd: LDS Church Archives.
Robert Pixton: Sheri E. Slaughter.
Mormon Battalion Ball: Museum of Church History and Art.
Orson Hyde: LDS Church Archives.
Winter Quarters: Jeanette Holmes Collection.
Plan of Winter Quarters: LDS Church Archives.
Lightning Storm: Scotts Bluff National Monument.

CHAPTER 3
1846 Mitchell map of western United States: University of Utah, Special Collections.
John Taylor: LDS Church Archives.
Norton Jacob: LDS Church Archives.
First pioneer women of Utah: LDS Church Archives.
The Pioneers: Stenhouse, *Rocky Mountain Saints.*
Appleton Milo Harmon: Utah State Historical Society.
Appleton Milo Harmon diary, 1847: LDS Church Archives.
Independence Rock: Scotts Bluff National Monument.

Mitchell Pass: Scotts Bluff National Monument.

Chimney Rock: Museum of Church History and Art.

White Men Killing Buffalo: Scotts Bluff National Monument.

Howard Egan: LDS Church Archives.

Amasa Lyman (1813–1877), Mormon apostle: LDS Church Archives.

Native American: LDS Church Archives.

Encampment on the Platte River: The Anschutz Collection.

Wilford Woodruff: LDS Church Archives.

Fording the Platte River: LDS Church Archives.

Jim Bridger: LDS Church Archives.

Fort Bridger: Library of Congress.

Sam Brannan: LDS Church Archives.

Horace K. Whitney: Utah State Historical Society.

Orson Pratt: LDS Church Archives.

Echo Canyon: Scotts Bluff National Monument.

Erastus Snow: LDS Church Archives.

Entering the Great Salt Lake Valley: Museum of Art, Brigham Young University.

Patty Sessions: LDS Church Archives.

William Hyde: Utah State Historical Society.

First view of Great Salt Lake Valley from Big Mountain: Library of Congress.

The Emigrant Train Bedding Down for the Night: The Corcoran Gallery of Art.

CHAPTER 4

Covered Wagons: Nebraska State Historical Society.

Willard Richards, his wife Jennetta, and their son Heber John: LDS Church Archives.

Latter-day Saints' Emigrant Guide: LDS Church Archives.

Salt Lake City: LDS Church Archives.

Mormon Battalion members: LDS Church Archives.

Emigration to the Western Country: Library of Congress.

Old Scout's Tale: Thomas Gilcrease Institute of American History and Art.

The Great Salt Lake of Utah: Library of Congress.

Buffalo Stampede: Scotts Bluff National Monument.

Margaret Gay Judd Clawson: Utah State Historical Society.

Crossing the South Platte: State Historical Society of Wisconsin.

Fort Laramie, June 24: State Historical Society of Wisconsin.

Crossing the Plains—Journeying Zionward: LDS Church Archives.

Prairie Burial: The Anschutz Collection.

Platte River near Fort Kearney: Scotts Bluff National Monument.

Devil's Gate: Library of Congress. Lee-Palfrey Collection. Manuscript Division.

Nelson Whipple: LDS Church Archives.

George A. Smith: LDS Church Archives.

George Mayer: Utah State Historical Society.

Heber C. Kimball: LDS Church Archives.

Buffalo Crossing the Missouri River: Thomas Gilcrease Institute of American History and Art.

Notice to emigrants: LDS Church Archives.

Emigrants moving to the West: Utah State Historical Society.

CHAPTER 5

Emigrants Crossing the Plains: Library of Congress.

Brigham Young: Special Collections, University of Utah.

Elk Horn Ferry: LDS Church Archives.

Ezra T. Benson: LDS Church Archives.

Jedediah M. Grant: LDS Church Archives.

Missionaries in Great Britain: LDS Church Archives.

Perpetual Emigration Fund promissory note: LDS Church Archives

The Mississippi at New Orleans: Library of Congress.

On board an emigrant ship: Library of Congress.

Aerial view of 1860 Boston: Library of Congress.

Iowa City: Library of Congress.

The Handcart Company: Museum of Church History and Art.

Edmund Ellsworth: Utah State Historical Society.

Edward Bunker: LDS Church Archives.

Mormon Emigrants Building Handcarts: Stenhouse, *Tell It All.*

Edward Martin and unidentified polygamous wife: LDS Church Archives.

Handcart train in a snowstorm: William W. Slaughter.

Martin Handcart Company: Museum of Church History and Art.

Devil's Gate: Museum of Church History and Art.

Hand-cart Emigrants in a Storm: Stenhouse, *Rocky Mountain Saints.*

Journal of James G. Bleak: LDS Church Archives.

Fort Bridger: Library of Congress.

Thomas L. Kane: LDS Church Archives.

James G. Bleak: Utah State Historical Society.

Journal of James G. Bleak: LDS Church Archives.

CHAPTER 6

Utah "Mountain Boys": LDS Church Archives.

Joseph W. Young: LDS Church Archives.

Old Tabernacle and bowery, Temple Square, Salt Lake City: LDS
  Church Archives.
Oxen, wagons, and teamsters at Echo Canyon: LDS Church Archives.
George Q. Cannon: Utah State Historical Society.
The Rough and Ready Boys: Utah State Historical Society.
John R. Murdock: LDS Church Archives.
Approaching Chimney Rock: Scotts Bluff National Monument.
Wagons fording a river: Nebraska State Historical Society.
Emigrants, Needle Rocks: Nebraska State Historical Society.
Unidentified pioneer children: LDS Church Archives.
Down-and-back wagon train: LDS Church Archives.
The dock at Plymouth, England: LDS Church Archives.
Emigrant Ship: Museum of Church History and Art.
Emigrant Vessel—between Decks: Library of Congress.
William Wood: LDS Church Archives.
The Port of New York: Library of Congress.
Nebraska City, River Front from the Iowa Side: Nebraska State Historical
  Society.
Ira Eldredge: Utah State Historical Society.
Omaha, Nebraska: Nebraska State Historical Society.
Mormon trail encampment: Utah State Historical Society.
Pioneers fording the Platte River: Special Collections, University of
  Utah.
Sioux Indian village: Nebraska State Historical Society.
Wagon train: LDS Church Archives.
Pioneer Burial at Wolf Creek: Museum of Church History and Art.
George Teasdale: LDS Church Archives.
Mormon emigrants near Coalville: LDS Church Archives.
View of Great Salt Lake, 1867: Library of Congress.
Salt Lake Tabernacle: LDS Church Archives.
Brigham Henry Roberts: LDS Church Archives.
The railroad reaches the 100th meridian: Library of Congress.
American Fork Brass Band: LDS Church Archives.

CHAPTER 7
Union Pacific Rail Road poster: Lee Groberg.
Promontory, Utah: Utah State Historical Society.
Joining of the Union Pacific and the Central Pacific railroads: LDS
  Church Archives.
Indians in front of Zion's Cooperative Mercantile Institution: LDS
  Church Archives.
Looking south along Main Street, Salt Lake City: LDS Church
  Archives.

Brigham Young, his counselors, and the Quorum of Twelve Apostles:
  Utah State Historical Society.
Twenty-fourth of July parade: LDS Church Archives.
Wilford Woodruff: LDS Church Archives.
Pioneers of 1847: LDS Church Archives.

INDEX

Note: Page numbers in italics indicate a photograph or illustration.